# Spanish Cooking at Home and on Holiday

Maite Manjón was born in Madrid in 1931 and studied medicine at the University there before working for one of Spain's leading surgeons. While studying English in London, she met her husband, scriptwriter Jan Read, who wrote the original story of *The Blue Lamp* and many scripts for *Dr Finlay's Casebook*. Her interest in cooking dates from her marriage and she has had extensive practical experience in classical Spanish cuisine and in adapting Spanish dishes in England. She and her husband live in London and have one son.

Catherine O'Brien was born in Edinburgh in 1916 and her first job was with the British Library in Palma de Majorca. She has worked as publicity director on many well-known films including *A Man For All Seasons*, *Far From The Madding Crowd* and *Richard III*, made in Spain. She and her husband, Bill Batchelor, own a villa in Pollensa, Majorca. Her great interest is in Majorcan cooking and she has transcribed many of the traditional recipes which originate from that part of Spain.

# Spanish Cooking
## at Home and on Holiday

*Maite Manjón*
*and*
*Catherine O'Brien*

*Illustrations*
*by*
*Margaret Theakston*

A Pan Original

PAN BOOKS LTD: LONDON

First published 1973 by Pan Books Ltd,
33 Tothill Street, London, SW1.

ISBN 0 330 23512 5

*Printed in Great Britain by*
*Cox & Wyman Ltd, London, Reading and Fakenham*

# Contents

# International Conversion Tables

These conversion tables are intended to help all users of PAN cookery books – wherever they live in the world. The weights and measures used throughout this book are based on British Imperial standards and metric units. However, the following tables show you how to convert the various weights and measures simply.

## International Measures

| Measure | UK | Australia | New Zealand | Canada |
|---|---|---|---|---|
| 1 pint | 20 fl oz | 20 fl oz | 20 fl oz | 20 fl oz |
| 1 cup | 10 fl oz | 8 fl oz | 8 fl oz | 8 fl oz |
| 1 tablespoon | $\frac{5}{8}$ fl oz | $\frac{1}{2}$ fl oz | $\frac{1}{2}$ fl oz | $\frac{1}{2}$ fl oz |
| 1 dessertspoon | $\frac{2}{5}$ fl oz | no official measure | — | — |
| 1 teaspoon | $\frac{1}{5}$ fl oz | $\frac{1}{8}$ fl oz | $\frac{1}{6}$ fl oz | $\frac{1}{6}$ fl oz |

## Conversion of fluid ounces to metric

| | |
|---|---|
| 1 fl oz | = 2·84 millilitres |
| 35 fl oz (approx 1$\frac{3}{4}$ Imperial pints) | = 1 litre (1000 ml or 10 decilitres) |
| 1 Imperial pint (20 fl oz) | = approx 600 ml (6 dl) |
| $\frac{1}{2}$ Imperial pint (10 fl oz) | = 300 ml (3 dl) |
| $\frac{1}{4}$ Imperial pint (5 fl oz) | = 150 ml (1$\frac{1}{2}$ dl) |
| 4 tablespoons (2$\frac{1}{2}$ fl oz) | = 70 ml (7 centilitres) |
| 2 tablespoons (1$\frac{1}{4}$ fl oz) | = 35 ml (3$\frac{1}{2}$ cl) |
| 1 tablespoon ($\frac{5}{8}$ fl oz) | = 18 ml (2 cl) |
| 1 dessertspoon ($\frac{2}{5}$ fl oz) | = 12 ml |
| 1 teaspoon ($\frac{1}{5}$ fl oz) | = 6 ml |

(All the above metric equivalents are approximate)

## Conversion of solid weights to metric

2 lb 3 oz = 1 k (kilogram)
1 lb      = 453 gm (grammes)
12 oz     = 339 gm
8 oz      = 225 gm
4 oz      = 113 gm
2 oz      = 56 gm
1 oz      = 28 gm

## Equivalents

1 UK (old BSI standard) cup equals 1¼ cups in Commonwealth countries
4 UK tablespoons equal 5 Commonwealth tablespoons
5 UK teaspoons equal 6 New Zealand or 6 Canada or
  8 Australia
1 UK dessertspoon equals ⅔ UK tablespoon or 2 UK teaspoons

In British cookery books, a gill is usually 5 fl oz (¼ pint), but
in a few localities in the UK it can mean 10 fl oz (½ pint).

Other non-standardized measures include:
Breakfast cup = approx 10 fl oz
Tea cup       = 5 fl oz
Coffee cup    = 3 fl oz

## Oven temperatures

| Description | Electric Setting | Gas Mark |
| --- | --- | --- |
| Very cool | 225°F (110°C) | ¼ |
|  | 250°F (130°C) | ½ |
| Cool | 275°F (140°C) | 1 |
|  | 300°F (150°C) | 2 |
| Very moderate | 325°F (170°C) | 3 |
| Moderate | 350°F (180°C) | 4 |
| Moderately or | 375°F (190°C) | 5 |
| fairly hot | 400°F (200°C) | 6 |

| Description | Electric Setting | Gas Mark |
|---|---|---|
| Hot | 425°F (220°C) | 7 |
| | 450°F (230°C) | 8 |
| Very hot | 475°F (240°C) | 9 |

These temperatures are only an approximate guide as all ovens vary slightly, according to the make and country of manufacture.

# Preface

The doyen of Spanish chefs, Don Ignacio Doménech, at once the Mrs Beeton and André Simon of Spanish cookery, lays down various prerequisites for serving an agreeable meal as follows. The dining-room must be shaded and its outlook pleasant; ladies must be provided with cushions on which to rest their feet; and above all, the guests should be bidden five days in advance and must be punctual. These are counsels of perfection. Our aim is more modest: to provide a simple and practical guide for the many people who have acquired a taste for the piquant Spanish cuisine and wish to experiment with it.

Quite half the charm of a foreign holiday is to recall one's discoveries abroad, not least an unusual meal at a small restaurant or a bottle of wine that was as delicious as it was inexpensive. We have therefore tried to explain how some typical Spanish and Majorcan dishes may be made with ingredients available wherever you live. To taste *Greixera de Carne* (see page 67) or *Paella* (page 38) on a winter's night at home, preferably with a bottle of Rioja or Valdepeñas, is to recapture sunshine and blue sea and the tang of wood smoke in the air.

At a time when it is so popular to rent a villa or apartment in the Mediterranean, our second aim is to make suggestions for cooking and marketing when on holiday in Spain and the Spanish Islands. There are, of course, people who go abroad only to recreate a Little England or America; and the wily foreigner is quick to oblige with fish and chips, tomato ketchup and the ubiquitous *biftek*. We wish all such *buen apetito* – but it is not for them that we have written this book.

Practicality has been our watchword. All the recipes in the main body of the book have been tried – and work. Where special ingredients are included, suggestions are given for obtaining them. Quantities are given both in British and metric units.

We wish to thank our husbands for their patience – not always unfailing – during the birth pangs of the book, and one of them, Mr Jan Read, for writing the section on Spanish wines, which was prepared with advice from Don Antonio Larrea Redondo, Director of the Estación de Viticultura y Enología at Haro, and other Spanish experts.

To you, too – *buen apetito*!

# An Introduction to Spanish Cooking

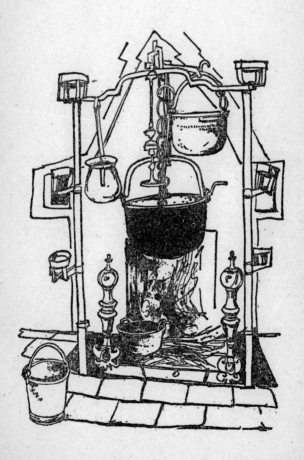

# Spanish Food at Home

When cooking some of the recipes at home, difficulty may arise in obtaining ingredients which are a commonplace in Spain.

This mainly applies to shellfish. More or less all of the fish mentioned, including from time to time inkfish and fresh sardines, are available from good fishmongers in larger towns. It is obviously sensible to plan your menu according to prevailing prices, although frozen Alaska king crab, frozen or canned prawns and potted shrimps are often a useful standby. Canned inkfish and freeze-dried *paella* are not usually to be recommended if you are used to the real thing, nor are preserved mussels in jars a satisfactory substitute for the fresh fish – except as an aperitif. (When using them for cooking it is virtually impossible to get rid of the taste of vinegar.)

Fresh green and red peppers and also aubergines (eggplant) can be bought from most greengrocers in season. At other times canned peppers are almost as good.

Pasta and dried vegetables, like saffron, Spanish and Italian rice and chick-peas, are obtainable at many of the larger supermarkets in Britain and elsewhere, as well as at delicatessens and specialized foreign grocers. Other locally obtainable varieties of dried beans are often a perfectly satisfactory alternative.

Olive oil is most economically purchased in large cans obtainable from the same sources.

It is difficult to find the best qualities of *chorizo* outside Spain, but a cheaper variety adequate for cooking is now making its appearance abroad. Other varieties of cured sausage and salami are generally not piquant enough to substitute, though a dark red French sausage from Provence containing hot paprika is now becoming available.

*A Note on Cooking Vessels.* Throughout the recipe section

there are frequent references to *cazuelas*, which are the earthenware casseroles used throughout Spain. Although they are available in other countries, a good substitute for them would be the excellent line of French casseroles which have become popular in recent years. Like *cazuelas*, these casseroles come in various sizes and can be used both for cooking and for serving. (For more details about *cazuelas*, see Chapter 13.)

# *The Importance of Olive Oil*

Olive oil is used almost exclusively as a cooking medium along the Mediterranean coasts and in Spain generally. There are various good reasons for this. It is cheap; if properly used it does not disappear into the food, leaving it heavy and fattening; it is healthier and less likely to cause thrombosis than animal products like lard and cooking fat; and a faint, but not overpowering flavour of olive oil is essential to some Mediterranean dishes.

The secret is to use good-quality oil and never to begin frying until it is really hot, with a faint vapour haze rising from the surface. It is also important to drain off any excess oil when cooking is finished. For example, when cooking onions and pimentos for a *salsa española* (see page 6), it does not matter how much oil is employed – but it is essential to tip the pan and drain off every drop of excess before adding the other ingredients. Again, when making a stew, any excess oil floating on the surface must be spooned off.

A bowl or empty jar should be kept handy, into which any surplus oil can be poured for further use. Important: do not mix oil used for cooking fish with oil used to cook other food.

If properly done, frying with olive oil is the best way to make food really crisp and leave it odourless.

There are many different grades of olive oil. The virgin oil produced from the first pressing of the olives is the best for making salad dressing, but is liable to smoke excessively if used for frying. It is most important that only a good-quality refined oil should be used for cooking.

If you are stuck with a strong-tasting olive oil, the best thing to do is to fry a slice of bread in it. This will remove the worst of the taste.

## *Garlic and Saffron*

First of all, leaving aside the question of flavour, recent research has shown that both garlic and onions possess most valuable medicinal properties, both antibiotic and in guarding against thrombosis – so that, if it tastes nasty, it is nevertheless good for you!

As to the flavour, the secret of cooking with garlic is moderation. When properly used, it enhances the taste of the food, and it is a safe bet that the most rabid garlic-hater – whatever he may say to the contrary – will never detect it.

When using garlic in salads, a squeezer is indispensable. *One* clove squeezed into a French dressing is plenty.

Squeezed garlic should be fried only briefly because it rapidly burns and blackens. If adding garlic in squeezed form to, say, *salsa española*, (see page 6) do so shortly before removing the pan from the fire. The other method of frying with garlic is to add the cloves, whole or coarsely sliced, earlier in the cooking and to remove them with a spoon afterwards. Again, be sparing with it and use too little rather than too much – one clove goes a long way.

Saffron is made from a cultivated crocus and bought in small packets containing the dried stamens. It is expensive in Spain and more so elsewhere, but is used in very small quantities. In recipes calling for 'a pinch of saffron', a few of the stamens should be ground in a mortar before use. A convenient and much cheaper substitute, especially for soups, is the prepared 'saffron powder'.

# PART ONE
# The Recipes

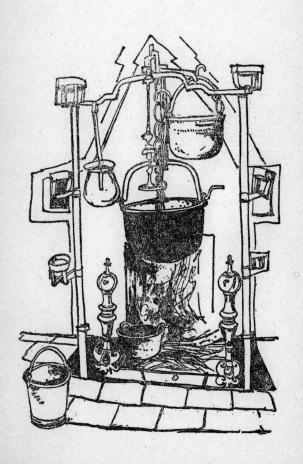

# 1
# *Sauces*

### Salsa Ali-oli *(o al ajo)*

Garlic Sauce

This sauce must be served with discretion since it appeals only to people who like garlic. It is delicious when served with fish cooked as a *bullavesa* or Spanish-style *bouillabaisse* and served separately from the broth. It is also excellent as a dip for shellfish.

Faced with a mixed party of garlic-lovers and garlic-haters, why not have one bowl of straightforward mayonnaise and one of garlic sauce? Then everyone will be happy!

4 tablespoons olive oil
3 cloves garlic,
  crushed

2 tablespoons parsley,
  chopped
Lemon juice

Put the olive oil in a mortar or blender, if you have one, add the garlic and parsley and blend or mix well with a little lemon juice. The *ali-oli* will thicken beautifully and smell delectable.

### Salsa Aurora

Dawn Sauce

½ pint (¼ litre) basic white
  sauce (see page 5)

4 tomatoes, peeled and sieved
Salt and pepper

Make the white sauce as described in the following recipe. Add the sieved tomatoes and blend well, adding salt and pepper to taste. This gives it the rosy flush from which it takes its name.

An excellent starter can be made by breaking an egg into a small *cazuela* or individual casserole, pouring the *salsa aurora* over it, and leaving on top of the stove until just set.

### *Salsa Béchamela*

Basic White Sauce

| | |
|---|---|
| 1 oz (25 gm) butter | Salt and pepper |
| 1 oz (25 gm) flour | ½ pint (¼ litre) milk |

Melt the butter in a small saucepan and stir in the flour. Cook carefully over a low heat until the butter and flour blend thoroughly without browning. Remove the pan from the heat, season with salt and pepper, then, on a low heat, add the milk gradually, stirring all the time so that the sauce does not get lumpy as it thickens.

This is the basic recipe for white sauce, which is made thicker or thinner by the use of less or more milk; it can be modified in endless ways – for example, by the addition of grated cheese or stock. In its thickest form it is the basis for croquettes made with meat, chicken or fish (see page 22).

Here is one of the more elaborate versions:

| | |
|---|---|
| 1 oz (25 gm) butter | 1 tablespoon thyme |
| 1 small onion, chopped | 1 tablespoon chopped parsley |
| 1 oz (25 gm) flour | or tarragon |
| ½ pint (¼ litre) mixed milk and chicken stock | 1 egg yolk |
| | Milk or cream |
| 1 bay leaf | Salt and pepper |

Melt the butter, stir in the chopped onion and cook gently for 2 to 3 minutes. Incorporate the flour as previously described and add the chicken stock and milk, also the herbs. Cook until the sauce thickens a little. Beat the egg yolk into a little milk or cream. Add to the sauce, stirring all the time. Season with salt and pepper to taste.

### *Salsa de Pimientos Rojos*

Red Pepper Sauce

| | |
|---|---|
| Olive oil | 1 small onion, finely chopped |
| 14 oz (400 gm) can red peppers | 1 clove garlic, crushed |

Put some olive oil in a pan and fry the onion slowly for about 10 minutes. Drain off the excess oil and add the crushed garlic. Cut the peppers into small pieces, cook very slowly with the onions for 10 to 15 minutes, then put the mixture through a blender or sieve.

This is delicious with lamb or other meat as a change from the traditional redcurrant jelly.

### Salsa Española (o Sofrito)

Frequently used and entirely characteristic of Spain, this sauce is not the same as the *Sauce Espagnole* of the French. Richard Ford, still the most reliable guide to things Spanish, although he wrote more than a hundred years ago, prints a remarkable testimonial to *salsa española*: 'It puzzles even the acumen of a Frenchman; for it is still the great boast of the town of Olvera that . . . they served up some donkeys as rations to a Buonapartist detachment . . .' He adds that 'to change this sauce would be little short of heresy' and that its *'negro de hueso* colour is the livery of tawny Spain, where all is brown from the *Sierra Morena* to duskier man. Of such hue is his cloak, his terra-cotta house, his wife, his ox, his ass, and everything that is his.'

Everything changes, everything flows, especially sauces – but *salsa española*, fortified by the addition of tomatoes, unknown to the Spaniards of Ford's generation, has lost none of its colour or its savour.

This purée of onions, red peppers and tomatoes (known as *sofrito* in Majorca), is therefore the basic Spanish sauce. It will be called for in conjunction with many of the dishes described in the book and we shall simply refer to the recipe given here.

| | |
|---|---|
| Olive oil | 1 clove garlic, crushed |
| 2 large onions, chopped | Salt and pepper |
| 2 fresh or canned red peppers, chopped | 1 glass dry sherry |
| 1 lb ($\frac{1}{2}$ kilo) tomatoes, or 14 oz (400 gm) can tomatoes | |

6

Pour a good quantity of olive oil into a large frying-pan. Add the onions and fry gently in the hot oil. When the onion is half cooked, add the peppers, removing the seeds if the peppers are fresh, and continue the slow frying for about 20 minutes until they are tender. Then tilt the pan, retaining the vegetables with a spoon, and drain off all the excess oil, which may be kept for further use. Once again spread the onions and peppers over the surface of the pan and add the tomatoes. Fry slowly until all the ingredients form a pulp, finally adding a crushed clove of garlic and salt and pepper to taste. Pass the mixture through a sieve or a blender and stir the sherry into it.

### Salsa Mahonesa

Mayonnaise

Mayonnaise is a truly Majorcan recipe since it is supposed to have originated in Mahon, capital of the Balearic island of Minorca, a short distance by sea from Majorca.

If you have a blender, a large quantity of mayonnaise can be made without danger of its thickening or curdling. It is simply a matter of adding oil until the desired consistency is obtained. The following amounts can be increased in proportion if a larger quantity is needed:

2 egg yolks
1 teaspoon mustard powder
1 teaspoon salt
1 clove of garlic, crushed
Juice of a lemon or equivalent
  amount of refined wine
  vinegar

Olive oil as required (roughly ½ pint or ¼ litre)

### Method with blender

Put the egg yolks, mustard, salt and garlic into the blender and mix at medium speed. Pour in olive oil at a trickle, still mixing at the same speed, until the mayonnaise has

7

thickened. Add the lemon juice or 1 tablespoon wine vinegar and blend at the highest speed for a few seconds.

Store in a screw-top jar in the refrigerator.

*Method without blender*

In a large bowl, crush the garlic into the 2 egg yolks. Incorporate the salt and mustard powder. Add the olive oil drop by drop, beating all the time with a wooden spoon until the mayonnaise is sufficiently thick. Should the mayonnaise threaten to curdle, whisk in another egg yolk. After the mayonnaise has thickened, trickle in the lemon juice or vinegar and stir well.

Some people prefer to leave the garlic out of the recipe, relying only on the oil, egg and lemon for flavour.

### Salsa Mahonesa Muselina

Fluffy Mayonnaise

Proceed as already described in the previous recipe for mayonnaise, but add the whites of the 2 eggs, beaten very stiff, after the ordinary mayonnaise has been beaten and has thickened.

This mayonnaise is particularly suitable for Russian salad (see page 89).

### Salsa para Pescado

Sauce for Fish

| | |
|---|---|
| 1 small can red peppers | 2 or 3 tomatoes, skinned |
| 3 cloves garlic | Salt |
| 1 small chilli (optional) | 2–3 tablespoons olive oil |
| 1 teaspoon paprika | 2–3 tablespoons wine vinegar |

Cut the red peppers into small pieces. Blend or grind in a

mortar with the garlic, a tiny bit of chilli (if used), paprika, tomatoes and a little salt, so as to make a fine paste. Blend in the olive oil and wine vinegar.

This makes a lovely sauce to accompany any fish, including lobster.

### Salsa Tártara

Tartare Sauce

Tartare sauce is a great favourite with the Majorcans, especially when served with fish or cold chicken. They make it simply by taking two cups or so of ordinary mayonnaise and stirring in a chopped hard-boiled egg, 12 capers, 3 or 4 finely chopped gherkins and, at the last moment, chopped chives or parsley.

### Salsa Vinagreta

Vinaigrette Sauce (French Dressing)

| | |
|---|---|
| 1 small clove garlic | ½ teaspoon prepared mustard |
| 2 tablespoons refined vinegar | ¼ teaspoon white pepper |
| ½ teaspoon salt | 4 tablespoons best olive oil |

Squeeze the garlic into the vinegar, mix in the salt, mustard, and pepper, then add the oil and stir vigorously until it forms an emulsion.

By *salsa vinagreta* the Spaniards frequently mean a French dressing as above, into which have been stirred:

| | |
|---|---|
| 2 chopped shallots | Chopped chives to taste |
| 2 tablespoons chopped parsley | |

This is often used in summer as an accompaniment to cold fish.

# 2
# *Soups*

### Bullavesa Mallorquina

Majorcan Fish Soup (*Bouillabaisse*)

*Serves 4*

| | |
|---|---|
| Olive oil | 2 lb (1 kilo) white fish |
| 4 oz (100 gm) spring onions | Salt |
| 2 tablespoons parsley, chopped | Pinch fennel |
| | Pinch thyme |
| 4 oz (100 gm) tomatoes, skinned and chopped | Pinch tarragon |
| | 1 teaspoon saffron powder |
| 2 cloves garlic | Croûtons of fried bread |
| 1 stick celery, chopped | (see page 15) |

Cover the bottom of a deep earthenware pot or large *cazuela* with olive oil and heat. Fry the onions, parsley, tomatoes and garlic for 15 minutes; season with salt to taste.

Add 2 pints (1 litre) water. Bring to the boil, add the celery, fennel, thyme and tarragon. Now add the fish and simmer for 20 minutes. Remove it with a draining spoon and take out the bones. Return the fish to the broth, add the saffron. Reheat gently and serve in soup plates with croûtons on the side.

### Consomé con Yema

Consommé with Yolk of Egg

A very popular starter, this consists simply of piping hot beef consommé with a raw egg yolk floating in each bowl.

### Gazpacho

Cold Summer Soup

*Serves 6*

This ice-cold soup originated in Andalucía and is popular

throughout Spain during the long hot summer – not least with foreign visitors.

It should be made in a big bowl, since any that remains is always welcome for another meal, but must be covered with a plate or foil to prevent everything else in the refrigerator from acquiring its piquant flavour.

| | |
|---|---|
| 14 oz (400 gm) can tomato juice | 1 small shallot, chopped |
| 2 tomatoes, skinned and chopped | Salt |
| 1 large cucumber, peeled and chopped | 1 large clove garlic, crushed |
| 2 green peppers, deseeded and chopped | 2 teaspoons paprika |
| | 1 teaspoon cumin seeds |
| | 3 tablespoons wine vinegar |
| | 1 tablespoon olive oil |

Pour the tomato juice into a large bowl, together with water measured by filling the empty can four times. If you have a blender you can save time by using it to chop the vegetables in some of the liquid – but be careful to stop before reducing them to a purée. With the amounts given, it will be necessary to put the vegetables through the blender in batches.

Now put all the chopped vegetables into the bowl with the liquid. Use of a blender results in a white foam, which must be removed with a spoon before seasoning. Add a little salt, the crushed or minutely chopped garlic, and the paprika first mixed in a little water. Pound the cumin seeds in a mortar. Add to the soup. Finally, stir in the vinegar, cover, and put in the refrigerator to cool. Just before serving, add a tablespoon of refined olive oil, stirring well again.

Many recipes for *gazpacho* include breadcrumbs, which are sometimes served separately in restaurants; but ordinary breadcrumbs form a glutinous mass in the soup and in our opinion are best left out.

### Sopa de Majillones

Mussel Soup

*Serves 2*

This is not strictly a Spanish recipe, since it calls for cream, which is in short supply along the Mediterranean. However, it was inspired by a holiday there and devised by an American film producer whose cooking is as good as his movies.

2 pints (1 kilo) mussels
Butter
2 shallots, finely chopped
½ pint (¼ litre) cream, single
  and double mixed

1 glass white wine
1 tablespoon parsley, chopped

Wash, clean and scrape the mussels, discarding any that are open (see pages 51–2). Put them in a pot with a little cold water and bring to the boil until they open. Remove from the shells and place on a plate.

Melt a little butter in a saucepan and fry the finely chopped shallots for about 10 minutes, slowly and without browning. Add the cream and mussels, stir, and keep on a low flame until heated through. Pour a little white wine into each soup cup, add the mussels in their sauce and sprinkle with the chopped parsley.

### Sopa de Cebolla Española

Spanish Onion Soup

*Serves 4*

2 pints (1 litre) chicken broth
1 lb (½ kilo) onions
Olive oil
1 oz (25 gm) butter
1 tablespoon caster sugar

1 glass dry white vermouth
Salt
Small bread cubes
2 oz (50 gm) grated cheese

If necessary, the chicken broth may be replaced by two chicken cubes dissolved in a similar quantity of water.

Cut the onions into rings and fry them slowly for about 30 minutes in a mixture of butter and an equal amount of olive oil until really soft. Remove from the heat when ready and sprinkle the caster sugar over them. Raise the heat and caramelize the onions quickly.

Transfer the onions to the pot containing the chicken broth. Add the vermouth and salt to taste. Leave the soup to simmer for about 1 hour and 30 minutes with the lid a little tilted so that some of the steam can escape.

Shortly before serving, prepare croûtons by frying small cubes of bread in olive oil until golden brown. The croûtons and grated cheese are brought separately to the table so that people may sprinkle them as they wish into the piping hot soup.

### Sopa de Pescado

Shellfish Chowder

*Serves 4*

A mixture of prawns, crayfish,    1 teaspoon saffron powder
   mussels and clams    Salt and pepper
4 oz (100 gm) Sopa Juliana*

Wash and clean the shellfish, discarding any mussels or clams that remain open (see pages 51–2).

Boil the shellfish in 2 pints (1 litre) salted water for about 5 minutes. Remove them with a draining spoon and pour the broth into a clean pan, straining it through muslin to get rid of any grit that has escaped the original cleaning. Add the dried vegetables and boil for about 30 minutes until soft,

---

*Sopa Juliana* is a mixture of dried vegetables used for making soups and can be bought very cheaply in Spain. Most countries have their own variation.

finally returning the fish to the soup together with a little saffron, salt and pepper.

This makes a fragrant and warming soup for a chilly evening.

### Sopa de Pescado Pepe

Pepe's Fish Soup

*Serves 6*

| | |
|---|---|
| Olive oil | 2 tomatoes, peeled |
| 2 lb (1 kilo) mixed white fish (cod, hake or bream) | 1 teaspoon saffron powder |
| 8 oz (¼ kilo) shrimps | 2 oz (50 gm) rice, boiled separately |
| 8 oz (¼ kilo) mussels | 1 clove garlic, crushed |
| 2 onions, chopped | Pepper |

Put a little olive oil into a deep stewing-pan and fry the onions and tomatoes, adding the crushed garlic as they become soft.

Clean the shrimps and mussels (see pages 51–2), boil them in 2 pints (1 litre) of water and strain the liquid through muslin to remove grit. Peel the shrimps and remove the mussels from their shells.

Simmer the white fish in the stock for 20 minutes, then remove with a draining spoon and bone it. Now add it to the fried vegetables in the stew-pan, together with the broth, the shellfish, the cooked rice and a little saffron powder.

### Sopa de Tomate

Tomato Soup

*Serves 4*

| | |
|---|---|
| 1 pint (½ litre) chicken broth | 1 onion, peeled and halved |
| 2 sticks celery, chopped | 3 or 4 lettuce leaves, coarsely chopped |
| 1 potato, peeled and halved | |

| | |
|---|---|
| 8 oz (200 gm) can peeled tomatoes | 3 sprigs parsley |
| 8 oz (200 gm) can tomato juice | 1 sprig rosemary |
| 1 teaspoon paprika | Salt and pepper |
| | 1 glass dry sherry |
| | 1 tablespoon chopped parsley |

Simmer the chicken stock with the vegetables, the herbs and seasoning for about 20 minutes. Remove the onion, rosemary and parsley, then pour the broth into a blender, in order to chop the other vegetables finely – without reducing them to a purée.

Put the tomatoes through a sieve, add the tomato juice and stir in the paprika.

Re-heat slowly and add the tomato mixture and sherry, and sprinkle with the chopped parsley.


### *Sopa de Uvas Blancas Malagueña*

Cold Grape Soup from Málaga

*Serves 4*

| | |
|---|---|
| 8 oz (200 gm) white grapes | 1 tablespoon vinegar |
| 20 almonds | 1 pint ($\frac{1}{2}$ litre) water |
| 3 cloves garlic | 2 oz (50 gm) fresh breadcrumbs |
| Salt | 6 ice cubes |
| 1 tablespoon olive oil | |

First skin the grapes and take out and discard the pips.

Warm the almonds in the oven, skin them, and pound in a mortar with the garlic and salt to taste. Stir in the oil gradually, mix well and then add the vinegar.

Transfer to a soup tureen, add the water, grapes, breadcrumbs and ice. Cool in the refrigerator for about an hour before serving.

This soup is also known in Málaga as *Ajo blanco con uvas* (Garlic with grapes). You have been warned!

## Sopa de Verdura Mallorquina

Majorcan Vegetable Soup

*Serves 4*

| | |
|---|---|
| 2 potatoes (optional) | 6 spinach leaves |
| 3 leeks | 2 sticks of celery |
| 1 large or 2 small turnips, sliced | 2 sprigs fresh tarragon |
| 2 or 3 carrots | 1 chicken stock cube |
| 1 small or half a large cabbage | Salt and pepper |
| | 1 clove garlic, crushed (optional) |

Boil the vegetables in 2 pints (1 litre) salted water to which a chicken cube has been added. When the vegetables are cooked (about 20 minutes) and the liquid reduced by about a third, put the contents of the pan through a sieve or blender. Add more salt if necessary, a little black pepper and – for those who like it – the garlic.

This soup can be varied by making it with any vegetables on hand – either raw or from a previous meal. It is a good way of using up cabbage and cauliflower stalks or celery sticks too robust for the cheeseboard. The potatoes make the soup thicker than it would be without them.

## Sopa Gaditana

There seems to be no English translation for this soup from Cadiz in the far south of Spain.

*Serves 6*

| | |
|---|---|
| 2 pints (1 litre) chicken broth | 3 eggs (two hard-boiled) |
| Olive oil | 1 tablespoon parsley, chopped |
| 5 oz (140 gm) ham | 1 glass dry sherry |
| 1 slice bread, cut in cubes | |
| 2 cloves garlic, crushed | |

Have a hot soup tureen ready. Heat the chicken broth. Fry the bread, the ham and garlic separately. Put them into the tureen as they are ready, together with the chopped hard-boiled eggs and the parsley. Separate the third egg, discard the white, stir the yolk with the sherry and add it to the tureen. Finally pour the boiling chicken broth over the mixture and serve immediately.

# 3
# Egg Dishes

*A Tortilla Española (Spanish Omelet)*

## Croquetas de Huevo

Egg Croquettes

*Serves 3*

The thick béchamel sauce described below can be used for croquettes with shellfish or minced chicken instead of hard-boiled eggs. Small croquettes made, for example, with frozen shrimps make an attractive starter or cocktail aperitif.

| | |
|---|---|
| 1½ oz (40 gm) butter | 1 egg, beaten |
| 3 tablespoons flour | Salt |
| 1 pint (½ litre) milk | Breadcrumbs |
| 4 hard-boiled eggs, chopped | Olive oil |

Melt the butter in a saucepan. Stir in the flour and add the milk little by little, so as to make a thick paste. Take the pan from the heat and mix in the hard-boiled eggs and salt to taste. Allow the mixture to cool, transfer to the refrigerator. Shape into croquettes between two spoons, finally dip in beaten egg and breadcrumbs and fry in hot olive oil until golden brown.

## Huevos a la Flamenca

Eggs Flamenca

*Serves 2*

All the colours of a Mediterranean sunset, this dish tastes as hot as it looks. It is a household word in Spain and is always cooked and served straight from the fire in a small *cazuela*.

2 onions, sliced
Olive oil
4 oz (100 gm) bacon,
   chopped
2 or 3 tomatoes, peeled and
   sliced
Salt and pepper
4 oz (100 gm) *chorizo* (see
   page 131)

1 small can red peppers, cut
   in strips
4 oz (100 gm) peeled prawns
   (fresh, or frozen and
   defrosted)
1 or 2 eggs per person

Fry the onions in olive oil until tender. Drain off the oil, add
the bacon and tomatoes and continue frying for another 5 to
10 minutes. Season to taste. Remove the mixture with a
draining spoon and divide it among 2 small *cazuelas* or
individual casseroles. Cut the *chorizo* into thin rounds and
place them around the edge of the dishes. Break the eggs
into the middle and cook fast on top of the stove so that the
whites are set and the yolks soft. At the last moment add
the prawns and arrange the strips of red peppers around the
top.

All the preparation may be done in advance, apart from
the final addition of the eggs, prawns and peppers before
serving.

*Huevos Revueltos con Tomate*

*Serves 2*

No exact translation exists for this blend of tomatoes and
egg, which is neither scrambled nor yet cooked like an
omelet. In a country where the British eggs and bacon are
exotic, it is popular both as a breakfast dish or for an
impromptu lunch or supper.

4 eggs
3 tomatoes

Salt and pepper
Butter or olive oil

Place the tomatoes in boiling water. Cool under the tap and

peel. Transfer them to a bowl and mash with a fork. Break the eggs into it and season with salt and pepper.

Heat a knob of butter or a little olive oil in a frying-pan until smoking. Pour in the mixture and stir vigorously with a fork until set.

### Nidos de Huevo

Egg Nests

*Makes 4 nests*

This is an off-beat lunch or supper dish or starter. But, as with many egg dishes, the final cooking must be done when the guests are at table.

| | |
|---|---|
| 1 lb ($\frac{1}{2}$ kilo) potatoes | Grated nutmeg |
| Milk | 1 shallot, finely chopped |
| Butter | 1 egg per nest |
| Salt | Olive oil |

Prepare some mashed potato a day beforehand with milk and butter. Season it with nutmeg and salt to taste. Pass through a sieve and leave in the refrigerator until required.

Next day, mix the shallot into the potato and shape the mixture into small snowballs, making a hollow in the middle with your knuckles. When all the nests are ready, break an egg yolk into each and set carefully on a kitchen board or other flat surface.

Heat a flat serving dish in the oven.

Put the separated egg whites into a bowl and beat until firm but not rigid. Heat some olive oil in a frying-pan until smoking. Cook the nests one at a time, lifting them carefully with a fish slice, passing them through the beaten egg white and then straight into the hot oil. Baste once with the hot oil, adjusting the flame so that by the time the yolk is soft-cooked the outside of the nest turns golden.

Place one by one onto the heated dish and serve on hot plates.

*Piperada Vasca*

Basque Omelet

*Serves 2*

More akin to scrambled eggs than an omelet proper, this dish, with its aromatic flavour of peppers, is popular in the villages on both sides of the Pyrenees.

If the mixture is prepared in advance, cooking can be completed in just two or three minutes before serving.

Olive oil
1 very large or two
  medium-sized onions,
  chopped
4 oz (100 gm) lean bacon or
  ham

4 tomatoes or 1 small can
  tomatoes
1 small can red peppers
Salt and pepper
3 eggs

Heat the oil in a frying-pan and fry the onions until half-cooked and tender. Drain off the excess oil. Cut up the bacon with scissors, mix with the onion and continue frying slowly for another 5 to 10 minutes. (If Bayonne ham or *jamón serrano* is used – which will give an even more piquant flavour – it is added later with the peppers). Peel and chop the tomatoes and cut the peppers into strips. Add to the onion mixture, together with the juice from the peppers and salt and pepper, and fry for a further 30 minutes on the lowest possible heat until the whole mixture is soft – but without it being reduced to a pulp. Break the eggs into the pan, raise the flame, and stir well with a fork until all the ingredients are blended and the egg cooked, but not hard.

This is best served with a green salad and French dressing (see page 9).

### *Tortilla de Champiñón*

Mushroom Omelet

*Serves 3*

Little olive oil or knob of
  butter
4 oz (100 gm) mushrooms,
  sliced
2 oz (50 gm) cooked ham,
  chopped

1 teaspoon chopped parsley
6 eggs
Salt and pepper

Heat the oil or butter in a frying-pan, add the mushrooms, chopped ham and parsley, cooking slowly for about 10 minutes until the mushrooms are done. Remove the mixture with a draining spoon and set aside on a hot plate.

Proceed now as for Brain Omelet (see below), cooking it only on one side and folding the mixture into the centre.

### *Tortillas Variadas*

Other Omelets

The above type of omelet can be made with a variety of fillings, such as prawns, green peppers, a mixture of fried mushrooms and onions, asparagus tips, and so on.

### *Tortilla de Sesos*

Brain Omelet

*Serves 3*

In Spain, brains should *not* be bought in the market, but only from a good butcher.

2 sheep's brains
Vinegar
1 bay leaf

Salt and pepper
6 eggs
Knob of butter

Soak the brains in salted water and vinegar for 20 minutes, then wash well and remove the membranes. Put the brains in a pan with cold water to cover, together with a bay leaf and a little salt, and bring to the boil, then reduce the heat and simmer slowly for 15 to 20 minutes, depending on size. Drain and cover (this keeps them white).

Beat the eggs in a bowl with a pinch of salt and pepper. Melt the butter in an omelet pan, and when it begins to smoke pour in the egg mixture. Cook only on the bottom side and place the brains on the top, folding over the omelet as if stuffing a pancake. Serve at once.

### Tortilla Española

Spanish Omelet

*Serves 4*

Spanish Omelet is a favourite item on the menus of restaurants all over the world. If you order it, the likelihood is that you will be brought a flat pancake in which are embedded strips of red or green peppers, pieces of tomato, peas and other vegetables.

This is not at all what the Spaniards themselves understand by a *tortilla*, eaten in every Spanish household at least once a week.

In Spain, *tortilla* means a thick round omelet containing only eggs, potato and onion. It is, in fact, a completely different dish from the French omelet which is made by cooking a thin film of egg against the hot metal of a pan, folding and serving with all speed.

| | |
|---|---|
| 4 large potatoes | Salt |
| 1 large onion | 6 eggs |
| Olive oil | |

First dice and mix the potatoes and onion. Heat a little olive oil in a large frying-pan, add the mixture, sprinkle with salt and fry slowly for about 20 minutes until soft but not crisp. Meanwhile, beat the eggs in a bowl with the addition of a little salt.

Remove the cooked potato and onion with a draining spoon and stir into the egg mixture.

Pour off all but a little of the oil from the frying-pan, leaving about as much as you would use for a French omelet. If there is any potato sticking to it, then the pan must be washed and dried and fresh oil added for the next stage. Heat briskly until the oil is smoking hot, then pour the egg and vegetable mixture into the pan, shaking all the time so that it does not stick to the bottom. Cook briefly, then remove from the fire and slide the omelet on to a large plate so that the uncooked side is still upwards. Place another plate on top and invert it. With the uncooked side now downwards, slide the omelet back into the pan and cook for another 2 or 3 minutes, shaking as before, to brown the second side.

The end result should be a cake about ¾-inch thick, crisp on both sides, but soft and succulent in the middle.

It is important to stick to the procedure for reversing the omelet during cooking or you will be involved in a Keystone Comedy situation, with sections of *tortilla* smoking acridly on the stove while you slither about the floor on the rest of the half-cooked onion and potato.

A large *tortilla*, accompanied by a green salad or a tomato salad with French dressing, makes a good main dish for an informal supper. Alternatively, small *tortillas*, cooked individually in a small pan, are an attractive starter. Eaten cold in buses, trains and the fields by the Spanish peasants, a *tortilla* is also a useful stand-by for a picnic.

### Tortillitas de Bonito con Tomate y Béchamel

Stuffed Tuna Omelet in two sauces

*Serves 4*

½ pint (¼ litre) white sauce
   (see page 5)
4 oz (100 gm) grated cheese
6 eggs

7 oz (175 gm) can tuna or
   salmon
½ pint (¼ litre) *salsa española*
   (see page 6)
Butter

Make a thin white sauce, stir in the cheese and pour half of it over the bottom of a shallow oven dish.

Beat the eggs and, in a separate bowl, mash the tuna with a tablespoon or two of *salsa española*.

Next, heat a little butter in a frying-pan until it smokes. Add a tablespoon of the egg mixture and as it spreads and cooks, put on top of it a spoonful of the seasoned tuna. Even this out, then fold the finished omelet like a pancake and place it in the cheese sauce. Make as many small omelets as the quantities of egg and fish mixture will allow. It is best to make a single layer of the omelets in the sauce; but if necessary they can be laid carefully on top of one another.

Pour the remainder of the cheese sauce over the top, then take a good quantity of *salsa española*, and spoon it between the little omelets so that it forms a criss-cross pattern in red across the whole surface. Finish by pouring more of the sauce right round the edge of the dish. Cook further in a moderately hot oven (400°F, Mark 6) for 15 minutes.

This dish is as decorative as it is delicious.

# 4
# *Rice and Pasta*

*Paella on the beach*

*Arroz Antonia*

Risotto Antonia

*Serves 6*

In Spain a picnic is by no means a casual meal. It is usually a grand family affair on Sundays or feast days.

The party, consisting of Grandma and Tía Antonia in addition to Father and Mother, the baby and five older children, pack into a small car, together with a *paellera*, eggs, rice and fish in plastic bags, yards of fresh bread, wine by the litre, a transistor radio and a portable butane gas cooker.

If possible, they settle by a convenient farmhouse as a base for operations. Otherwise cooking proceeds in the open – on the cooker or over a brushwood fire.

A favourite dish for such occasions is a *paella* (see also page 38). This is Tía Antonia's Majorcan version for 6 people – and very good it tastes after the long wait in the open air!

| | |
|---|---|
| 2 inkfish (optional) | 4 oz (100 gm) fresh or frozen |
| ½ lb (¼ kilo) chicken pieces | peas |
| Olive oil | Salt and pepper |
| 2 onions, sliced | Chicken stock cube |
| ½ lb (¼ kilo) pork fillet, | 1 teaspoon saffron powder |
| sliced in rounds | Rice (1 cup per person) |
| 2 oz (50 gm) *chorizo*, sliced | 2 hard-boiled eggs, sliced |
| (see page 131) | 8 oz (200 gm) frozen prawns |
| 2 oz (50 gm) chopped ham | 4 canned red peppers, cut in |
| 2 tomatoes, peeled and | strips |
| chopped | |

Start by cleaning the inkfish (squid) and cutting it into rings (see page 47). Then fry the chicken. Both of these preparations can be done in advance, especially if you wish to cook this dish out of doors.

Now put some olive oil into a *paellera* or large frying-pan and fry the onions until they are half-cooked. Add the pork and cook for about 3 minutes longer. Then add the chicken,

32

*chorizo*, ham, inkfish, tomatoes and peas. Stir thoroughly and season to taste.

Make some stock with the chicken cube, allowing two cups of liquid for one of rice, and flavour it with the saffron. Add this to the contents of the pan, together with the rice. Stir well and cook slowly for 18 minutes. Finally add the sliced, hard-boiled eggs, the prawns and strips of red pepper. Simmer for a further 5 minutes.

### *Arroz Azafranado*

Saffron Rice

*Serves 3*

8 oz (200 gm) rice
Salt
Olive oil
2 tomatoes, peeled

1 small onion, chopped
1 clove garlic, crushed
1 pinch saffron

Boil the rice in salted water in the usual way. Fry the onion and tomatoes with the garlic and saffron. Remove with a draining spoon and mix with the hot, drained rice.

An alternative method is to add the saffron to the salted water in which the rice is boiled.

### *Arroz con Pescado*

Fish Risotto

*Serves 2*

1 lb (½ kilo) fresh tuna,
  smoked haddock or canned
  salmon
Pinch thyme
1 teaspoon parsley, chopped
1 bay leaf
Lemon juice

Salt
4 oz (100 gm) rice
4 oz (100 gm) butter
3 tomatoes, peeled, chopped
  and sieved
2 hard-boiled eggs, chopped

Cut the tuna into slices and simmer for about 10 minutes in a little salted water with thyme, parsley and a bay leaf. If using haddock, poach it in a little milk and water until tender, remove skin and bones and mash with a fork. Canned salmon requires no prior preparation except mashing after the removal of any discoloured skin.

Boil the rice for 20 minutes in ½ pint (¼ litre) water to which a little lemon juice and salt have been added. When cooked, drain and mix the rice with the fish, stirring in the butter and puréed tomato. Add the chopped, hard-boiled eggs and serve piping hot.

### *Arroz Con Riñones Maria*

Maria's Rice with Kidneys

*Serves 2*

| | |
|---|---|
| 1 lb (½ kilo) kidneys | 4 oz (100 gm) rice |
| Salt and pepper | 4 oz (100 gm) cooked ham, |
| 2 onions, sliced | chopped |
| 1 clove garlic, crushed | 1 tablespoon parsley, |
| Juice of 1 lemon | chopped |
| 1 glass sherry | Olive oil |

Treat the kidneys as for the recipe on page 72, then slice them and put them in a shallow dish with half the onion, the garlic, ground black pepper, a little salt, the lemon juice, sherry and parsley. Allow to marinate for an hour.

Meanwhile, boil the rice and keep it warm in a low oven. Fry the remaining onion in olive oil until tender and drain off the excess oil. Add the kidneys and the marinade, together with the chopped ham, and cook for a further 15 minutes.

Finally, take the rice out of the oven and pour the mixture over it.

### Coca Mallorquina

Majorcan Pie

*Serves 4*

A Majorcan version of the Italian *pizza*, this consists of a large pastry case with a savoury filling.

In Majorca, where the oven, whether fired by the traditional charcoal, butane gas or electricity, is generally difficult to control, people often ask the local baker to cook this dish for them!

*Pastry*

½ lb (¼ kilo) plain flour          4 tablespoons olive oil
½ teaspoon salt

Sieve the flour and salt into a bowl. Make a well in the middle and add 4 tablespoons of water and the oil. Whisk the mixture lightly for about a minute, then knead it on a floured board and roll it out. Line a large round tin and bake in a moderately hot oven (375°F, Mark 5) for 15 to 20 minutes.

*Filling*

1 lb (¼ kilo) spinach
1 large onion, sliced
1 clove garlic, crushed
1 red pepper, deseeded and
  chopped
3 tomatoes, peeled and
  chopped
3 tablespoons olive oil

Salt and black pepper
2 oz (50 gm) fresh
  breadcrumbs
2 eggs (1 hard-boiled)
2 oz (50 gm) grated cheese
1 can anchovies, drained
12 black olives, stoned and
  chopped

Cook and drain the spinach and chop finely. Fry the onion, garlic, red pepper and tomatoes in olive oil until tender. Season, add the breadcrumbs, spinach, 1 chopped, hard-boiled egg, and finally stir in a raw egg.

Fill the pastry case with this mixture, spreading it well

over the surface. Sprinkle on the cheese and scatter the anchovies and olives at random over the top.

Cook in a moderate oven (350°F, Mark 4) for 15 to 20 minutes until set. Eat cold.

### Empanadillas

Spanish Pasties

*Serves 4*

This is a Spanish dish which looks like a Cornish pasty – but tastes completely different and is more piquant.

Both the pastry and the filling can be made several hours before serving.

### Pastry

| | |
|---|---|
| 1 lb (½ kilo) flour | Salt |
| 6 oz (150 gm) butter | 4 tablespoons dry sherry |

Sieve the flour into a bowl, make a well in the middle, add the butter, a pinch of salt and the sherry with two tablespoons of water (or a little more, if necessary). Knead together thoroughly. Cover and leave in the bowl for an hour or longer.

### Filling

| | |
|---|---|
| Olive oil | 2 or 3 fillets smoked haddock |
| 1 large onion, chopped | (or similar fish) |
| 4 large tomatoes, peeled and chopped | 8 oz (200 gm) cooked lean ham, chopped |
| 1 green pepper, deseeded and chopped | |

Cover the bottom of a frying-pan with olive oil. Into it put the onion, tomatoes and green pepper. Fry slowly until soft.

Meanwhile poach the fish in milk. Then bone and skin it, and mix with the chopped ham. Add to the vegetable mixture, cook together for 10 minutes and put aside on a plate.

Roll out the pastry on a floured surface. Place a heaped tablespoon of the filling on the pastry, away from the edge. Cut the surrounding pastry in a circle shape with a pastry wheel or sharp knife, leaving sufficient border to fold over the filling in the shape of a pasty.

Repeat this as long as you have filling and pastry, rolling out the pastry again when all the large areas have been used up. Put the pasties on a large floured serving dish or board until you are ready to fry them.

About 30 minutes before serving the *empanadillas*, heat a good quantity of olive oil in a large frying-pan. Put the pasties into the sizzling oil, basting until golden brown, so as to avoid turning them over. With the amounts given it will be necessary to cook them in batches.

You will be surprised at how many of these *empanadillas* your guests can manage. (Our friends' average is three each.) Serve them with a green salad.

### *Fideos Secos*

Majorcan Vermicelli

*Serves 2*

| | |
|---|---|
| 1 chicken stock cube | 8 oz (200 gm) tomatoes, |
| 8 oz (200 gm) vermicelli | peeled and chopped |
| 1 onion, chopped | 2 oz (50 gm) parsley, chopped |
| Olive oil | Salt and pepper |

Dissolve the chicken stock cube in hot water, boil the vermicelli for 20 minutes and drain. Fry the chopped onion in olive oil until golden but not crisp. Add the tomatoes, parsley, ham and mix with vermicelli. Season to taste and heat thoroughly before serving.

## Paella

We shall not attempt a translation because by now *paella* is as well known and as representative of Spain as is haggis of Scotland.

It is not difficult to obtain suitable ingredients, wherever you live, because *paella* is many things. In Valencia, where it originated, this saffron-tinted rice dish is made with chicken, meat, and small sausages. This may come as a surprise to those who think of it as an exotic confection of shellfish in the colours of the Spanish flag. In fact we believe that the best *paellas* are made without meat; but in most places, if only for reasons of economy, chicken is more or less indispensable. The Spanish make thrifty use of the dismembered chicken legs and thighs sold in the markets. But, of course, the results are better if you buy baby chickens or poussins and divide them up.

By the addition of extra rice a *paella* can be 'stretched' almost indefinitely – hence one of its attractions in a country of large families – but the wider the variety of the other ingredients, the more exciting it will be. It is therefore a dish for six or more, and certainly not less than four.

For *paella*, the best cooking utensil is a two-handled metal *paellera*. Failing this, a deep, good-sized frying-pan will do very well.

Here then, is one of the many variants:

*Serves 6*

| | |
|---|---|
| 2 poussins or 2 to 3 lb (1 to 1½ kilo) chicken | Rice ( 1 cup per person) |
| Flour | 1 pinch Saffron, |
| Olive oil | Shellfish – prawns, crayfish, lobster, crab |
| 1 lb (½ kilo) small inkfish (squid) | 1 large can red peppers, cut in strips |
| 2 pints (1 kilo) mussels | Green or black olives |
| Garlic | |

Inkfish is a most important ingredient and when cut up and distributed in the rice will not be noticed by people afraid of things with tentacles. Take your choice of the other shell-fish. It may be fresh or frozen; but preserved mussels are *not* suitable, since the vinegar ruins the flavour of the finished dish.

Cut up the chicken, dredge with flour and brown lightly in olive oil until tender. Put on a plate while preparing the other ingredients.

Clean the inkfish (see page 47), or get your fishmonger to do it. Cut into small pieces, fry in olive oil and put aside on another plate.

Scrape, clean and boil the mussels (see pages 51–2). Remove them from the shells, keeping the best half-shells for decoration. Strain the broth from the mussels through muslin to remove any particles of grit and keep for further use.

Put 2 tablespoons of olive oil into the *paellera* and fry two or three slices from a clove of garlic. When the garlic begins to brown, take it out and throw it away. Add the rice – preferably Spanish or Italian round rice and not the fluffy white, long-grained variety – in the proportion of one cupful per person. Fry gently until the rice begins to brown.

Meanwhile, grind together in a mortar a clove of garlic and a pinch of saffron. Scatter over the frying rice.

The total amount of liquid required for boiling the rice is two cupfuls per person, ie, exactly twice the amount of rice, made up from the strained mussel stock plus as much additional water as is needed. Add this now, stirring for 5 minutes as it begins to boil and bubble through the rice.

Stir in the inkfish and arrange the pieces of chicken around the outside of the pan in a circle.

When the rice, inkfish and chicken have cooked together for about 15 minutes, add the remainder of the ingredients decoratively on top of this mixture: first the various shell-fish, then strips of red pepper and the green or black olives.

Finally garnish with the mussels, replaced in the best of the half-shells in which they were cooked.

Turn off the heat and keep the *paella* covered with a clean tea cloth for about 7 minutes, when it will be ready to serve. (If you are using a frying-pan, this dish must obviously be served on individual dinner plates.)

# 5

## *Fish*

### Bacalao

A regular sight in any Spanish grocer's is the large, flat slabs of desiccated fish hanging from the ceiling. This is a variety of dried salted cod most popular in Spain – and even more so in Portugal. In itself, *bacalao* is about as appetizing as the pemmican dear to Fenimore Cooper; but it serves as the starting point for a variety of dishes with rich and piquant sauces, of which the best known is *Bacalao a la Vizcaina* – a household word in the north of Spain.

### Bacalao a la Vizcaina

*Serves 4*

| | |
|---|---|
| 2 lb (1 kilo) *bacalao* | ½ pint (¼ litre) *salsa* |
| Flour | *española* (see page 6) |
| Olive oil | 2 red peppers, blanched, |
| 2 chillis (optional), soaked | deseeded and sliced |
| for 2 hours | 1 tablespoon parsley, |
| 2 cloves garlic | chopped |
| 1 slice fried bread | 2 oz (50 gm) breadcrumbs |

Cut the *bacalao* into pieces and soak overnight. Before using it, place the fish in a saucepan with cold water and bring to the boil, removing and draining the pieces as the water shows signs of bubbling. Remove the bones, being careful not to break up the fish. Dip in flour and fry in olive oil until golden.

In a mortar, pound the chillis, garlic and the fried bread. Add this to the *salsa española*, stir well and pour half of the mixture into a shallow oven dish. Lay the pieces of fish in it and pour the remainder of the sauce over them. Decorate with strips of peppers, sprinkle the surface with a mixture of chopped parsley and breadcrumbs. Cook in a moderately hot oven (375°F, Mark 5) for 15 minutes.

### Bacalao al Horno

Bacalao Pie

*Serves 4*

2 lb (1 kilo) *bacalao*
Flour
4 tablespoons olive oil
2 onions, chopped
4 tomatoes, peeled and
  chopped
2 red peppers, deseeded
  and sliced

2 cloves garlic, crushed
2 oz (50 gm) breadcrumbs
8 oz (200 gm) mushrooms,
  sliced
Salt and pepper
Juice of $\frac{1}{2}$ lemon
1 lb 8 oz ($\frac{3}{4}$ kilo) mashed
  potato

Soak small pieces of *bacalao* in cold water overnight. Dry,
dip in flour and fry in olive oil until golden, then transfer to
an ovenproof dish.

In the same pan fry the onions, mushrooms, tomatoes and
peppers for about 15 minutes. Add the garlic, breadcrumbs,
mushrooms, lemon juice and salt and pepper to taste. Stir well,
then cover the fish with this mixture and top with the mashed
potato. Cook in a moderate oven (350°F, Mark 4) for about
an hour or until lightly browned.

### Bacalao con Salsa de Tomate y Cebolla

Bacalao with Tomato and Onion Sauce

*Serves 4*

2 lb (1 kilo) *bacalao*
Flour
Olive oil
14 oz (400 gm) can tomatoes

2 onions, chopped
1 clove garlic, crushed
Salt and pepper

Soak the *bacalao* overnight. Next day cut it into slices, dip
in flour, fry gently in a little olive oil and lay the slices on the
bottom of a shallow oven dish.

In the same pan, fry the chopped onions for 15 to 20 minutes and drain off the oil. Add the tomatoes, cook them for a further 10 minutes, then add the garlic and a little salt and pepper. Pour on top of the *bacalao* and put into a hot oven (425°F, Mark 7) for 15 minutes.

Serve with sauté potatoes.

### Bacalao en Molde

Bacalao Mould

1 lb (½ kilo) *bacalao*  
1 red pepper  
2 oz (50 gm) parsley  
Olive oil

1 small onion, chopped  
⅓ pint (200 ml or 2 dl) milk  
3 eggs, beaten

Soak the *bacalao* overnight.

Grill the red pepper, peel and remove the seeds. Mince the fish and parsley together.

Heat a little olive oil and fry the onion until tender. Remove the pan from the heat and add the milk and eggs. Add the *bacalao* mixture and pepper and stir well. Pour this into a well-greased mould. Place it in an oven dish half-filled with water and cook in a moderate oven (350°F, Mark 4) for 1 hour.

Serve with a fresh green salad or vegetable.

### Besugo al Horno

Baked Sea Bream (or Mackerel)

*Serves 2*

2 potatoes  
Olive oil  
1 bream or 2 mackerel  
1 lemon

Salt and pepper  
1 small glass dry sherry or  
white wine

Bream is popular in Spain and this is a traditional way of cooking it; but the recipe is equally suitable for mackerel. Both are oily fish which are improved by the addition of lemon and dry sherry.

Peel the potatoes, cut into thick slices and fry crisply in olive oil. Clean the fish, make two slits in the upper side and insert a slice of lemon in each. Line the bottom of a *cazuela* or casserole with the potato slices and place the fish on top. Squeeze the rest of the lemon over it, sprinkle with salt and pepper, and add the sherry or white wine. Cook in a moderate oven (375°F, Mark 4) for about an hour.

### *Besugo con Almendras a la Castellana*

Sea Bream with Almonds

*Serves 4*

| | |
|---|---|
| 1 large bream | 2 tablespoons parsley, |
| 1 lemon | chopped |
| 6 almonds | Salt and pepper |
| 1 large onion, sliced | 1 teaspoon cornflour |
| 1 tablespoon olive oil | |

Clean the fish, make a few slits in the sides and insert slices of lemon. Split the almonds in half and push them into the fish also. Place the fish in an ovenproof dish, cover with the onion and parsley, pour on the oil, season to taste, and put the dish, which should not be covered, into a moderate oven (350°F, Mark 4).

Cook for about 30 to 45 minutes or until golden. Transfer the fish to a hot serving dish and sprinkle the cornflour into the pan juices, boil for a minute or two, and pour over the bream.

### Boquerones

Fresh Anchovies

Fresh anchovies are quite distinct in taste from the canned variety. They are very easy to cook. Clean them, dip in seasoned flour and fry in smoking hot olive oil until crisp. As with whitebait, there is no need to bother about removing the bones.

Serve with fried parsley and slices of lemon.

### Calamares en su Tinta

Inkfish (Squid) in its Ink

*Serves 4*

| | |
|---|---|
| 2 lb (1 kilo) inkfish | Olive oil |
| 1 glass sherry | ½ pint (¼ litre) *salsa española* |
| Salt and pepper | (see page 6) |

This is a full-flavoured dish for the *aficionado* of Spanish cooking. Either you take to it or pale at the sight. It is as well to sample it at a restaurant before cooking it – and if you like it, to check that your guests share your taste!

The inkfish is cleaned as described in the following recipe, but the ink bags are retained for making the sauce. When cooking the dish in Spain, ask the fishmonger to give you a big inkbag from a large inkfish – this will avoid the fiddling business of extracting the bags from each small fish and will supply all that you need for the sauce. Squeeze the ink from the bag, or bags, through a sieve and into a cup, add the sherry and salt and pepper to taste, and mix well.

Slice the inkfish, fry for 5 minutes in olive oil, and then stew in *salsa española* for an hour.

The prepared ink is finally poured on top, giving the sauce the deep hue from which the dish takes its name.

### Calamares Fritos

Fried Inkfish (Squid)

*Serves 2 (or 4 as a starter)*

| | |
|---|---|
| 1 lb (½ kilo) inkfish | 1 egg, separated |
| 2 tablespoons flour | 2 teaspoons olive oil |
| 2 tablespoons milk | |

Buy no more than you need for immediate use. In Spain, be sure to ask for *calamares pequeños* (small inkfish), because the large ones have a rubbery consistency no matter how long they are cooked. Small inkfish on the other hand will always be tender with very little cooking.

Make the batter 1 hour 30 minutes before it is needed. Mix the flour, milk, egg yolk and oil until creamy. Before using it, and just before coating the inkfish, blend in stiffly beaten egg white. The same thin batter is also ideal for frying scampi.

To clean the fish, remove the head, the bag containing the ink and the body spine, then turn the inkfish inside out and wash them thoroughly. Cut into rings and coat with butter. Fry in hot olive oil and serve immediately.

### Calamares Rellenos

Stuffed Inkfish (Squid)

*Serves 4*

| | |
|---|---|
| 2 lb (1 kilo) inkfish | 2 oz (50 gm) *chorizo* |
| Olive oil | (optional) |
| 4 oz (100 gm) bacon or ham, chopped | ½ pint (¼ litre) *salsa española* (see page 6) |
| 4 oz (100 gm) tomatoes, peeled and sliced | Salt and pepper |

Use only the smallest inkfish. Clean them as described in the previous recipe, keeping the body whole. Chop the tentacles into small pieces. Heat a little olive oil and fry the bacon and tomatoes. If you have it, a little thinly sliced *chorizo* (see page 131) will give extra piquancy to the dish. Add the tentacles and salt and pepper to taste. Stuff the body or sac of the inkfish with this mixture. Stick a toothpick through the end to keep the stuffing inside and stew slowly in *salsa española* for about an hour. In Spain, where brandy is cheap, a little added to the sauce will improve it.

### Cangrejo con Salsa Picante

Crab in Piquant Sauce

*Serves 2*

| | |
|---|---|
| 8 oz (200 gm) crabmeat or other chunky shellfish | 1 teaspoon paprika |
| 2 oz (50 gm) butter | 2 oz (50 gm) grated cheese |
| 1 oz (25 gm) flour | 1 teaspoon brandy or dry sherry |
| ½ pint (¼ litre) milk | Salt |

This is made with fresh shellfish in Spain. If this is unavailable, frozen Pacific prawns, Alaska crab, scallops or lobster are all suitable and need no cooking except for the time that it takes to heat them in the sauce.

Make a thin white sauce (see page 5) with half the butter, the flour and milk. Stir in half the grated cheese, the paprika and the brandy or dry sherry.

Heat the shellfish in the sauce. Then divide into individual *cazuelas* or small fireproof dishes, cover the top with the rest of the cheese and dabs of the remaining butter and put under the grill to brown.

## Centollos a la Santanderina

Spider Crabs

*Serves 1*

Spider crabs or *centollos* differ from the British variety in possessing a flatter body and longer, more slender legs; and they are often smaller. They are eaten at their best in the sea-front restaurants of Santander in the north of Spain and along the Costa Cantábrica, where this recipe originates.

| | |
|---|---|
| 1 *centollo* | 1 tablespoon parsley, |
| Juice of ½ lemon | chopped |
| 1 tablespoon brandy | Freshly ground black pepper |
| 2 tablespoons dry white wine | Salt |

Clean the spider crab as you would an ordinary crab, being careful to remove and discard the 'dead men's fingers'.

Take off the top shell from the body and scoop out the meat, putting it in a pan with the lemon juice. Gently sauté, then pour over the brandy and flambé. Add the white wine and parsley and simmer slowly for about 10 minutes. Season to taste and put the mixture into the crab and replace the top shell to serve. Since spider crabs are not large, it is usual to serve one per person.

## Chanquetes

Whitebait

*Chanquetes* are a variety of tiny whitebait most abundantly fished off the coasts of Málaga. They are fried crisp like *Boquerones* (see page 46).

### Fritura Mixta de Pescados Pequeños

Mixed Fried Fish

*Serves 4*

In terms of fish, this corresponds to a mixed grill. It is obtainable in almost any Spanish restaurant and is a good choice if you are suffering from a surfeit of rich sauces. It is simplicity itself to cook, but requires a variety of different small fish, much more easily bought in a Spanish market than at home. (Ask the stall-holder in the market for 1 kilo of mixed small fish – '*un kilo de pescados pequeños mezclados*'.)

| | |
|---|---|
| 2 lb ( 1 kilo) of fish including the following (if obtainable): | *Boquerones* (fresh anchovies) |
| | *Calamares* (inkfish) |
| *Sardinas* (fresh sardines) | *Salmonetes* (red mullet) |
| *Gallos* ( a small fish of the turbot family) | Flour |
| | Olive oil |
| | Lemon segments |

Clean the fish, dredge with flour, and fry crisp in hot olive oil. Serve with segments of lemon.

The best accompaniment is a salad, either green or made from tomatoes or red or green peppers with French dressing.

### Gambas a la Plancha

Fried Prawns in Shell

*Serves 2*

| | |
|---|---|
| 1 lb (½ kilo) prawns in shell | 1 oz (25 gm) parsley, |
| 2 cloves garlic, crushed | chopped |

Put the prawns in a frying-pan with a little hot olive oil and fry slowly for 3 to 5 minutes until really hot. Add the crushed garlic and parsley. Serve immediately on hot plates.

This is a favourite *tapa*, or appetizer, in Spanish bars. The prawns are shelled and eaten with the fingers – so be sure to have finger bowls and lemon on hand.

### Gambas al Pil Pil (o al Ajillo)

Prawns with Hot Chillis

*Serves 2*

| | |
|---|---|
| Olive oil | 2 cloves garlic, crushed |
| 1 lb (½ kilo) fresh prawns or 4 oz (100 gm) frozen prawns | 2 or 3 *guindillas* (hot red chillis) |

Heat a little olive oil in separate small *cazuelas* or fireproof dishes. Add the prawns, peeled if they are fresh, the crushed cloves of garlic and the chillis, cut into small pieces. Cook briefly on top of the stove and serve in the *cazuelas*, so that it is piping hot when brought to the table.

This dish is best eaten by dunking fresh bread in the sauce.

Chillis are hot on the tongue, so reduce the quantity by half if you are not used to them.

### Mejillones de Aperitivo

Mussels for an Aperitif

| | |
|---|---|
| Mussels | Parsley |
| Shallots, finely chopped | Olive oil |
| 1 clove garlic, crushed | |

(The quantities vary, of course, according to the number of your guests and their appetites.)

Soak the mussels in a bowl of water, scrape the shells with a knife and scrub them until they are thoroughly clean. Discard any that are open.

Put the mussels in a large saucepan, with a little water, cover and bring to the boil, when the mussels will open. After cooking, discard any which do *not* open, as they are not fit to eat. Leave the mussels for a minute or two and then take them out with a draining spoon and put them on a plate. Remove the mussels from their shells, keeping enough of the half-shells for serving the mussels later. Meanwhile, make the sauce by frying together first the shallots, then the garlic and chopped parsley in a little olive oil.

Put the mussels into the clean half-shells and spoon the sauce over them. They are eaten by taking the shells in your fingers and sucking out the seasoned filling – and make an excellent cocktail snack or starter.

### *Merluza con Mahonesa y Salsa de Pimientos*

Hake with Mayonnaise and Sweet Pepper Sauce

*Serves 4*

| | |
|---|---|
| 2 lb (1 kilo) hake or halibut | 1 clove garlic, crushed |
| 1 onion, finely chopped | 2 shallots, finely chopped |
| Parsley, chopped | 1 large can red peppers |
| 1 glass white wine | ½ pint (¼ litre) mayonnaise |
| 2 tablespoons olive oil | (see page 7) |

Buy the hake or halibut in one piece. Wash it and put in a casserole with a little chopped onion and parsley, the white wine and olive oil. Cook for about 30 minutes in a moderately hot oven (400°F, Mark 6) – until the flesh comes off the bone easily.

Then make a sauce by sieving or blending more chopped parsley, along with the crushed garlic, shallots and the peppers. Bone the fish and replace it in the casserole. Pour over it first the mayonnaise and then the sauce and return it to the oven for 10 to 15 minutes to heat it throughout.

### Paquete de Pescado al Solterón

The Time and the Plaice (definitely for two)

*Serves 2*

Accustomed as he is to being waited on hand and foot, the Spanish Don Juan is not noted for culinary achievement – but Time Marches On – and this bachelor's dish will cook itself, in Spain or elsewhere, in the time it takes to deal with drinks for your guest.

| | |
|---|---|
| 4 fillets plaice or similar white fish | 4 oz (100 gm) mushrooms |
| 2 or 3 tomatoes, peeled and sliced | 2 oz (50 gm) butter |
| | Salt and pepper |

Lay a fillet of plaice on a piece of cooking foil. Dot with knobs of butter and a quarter of the mushrooms and tomatoes. Season with salt and pepper, then place the second fillet on top and proceed by making a layered sandwich of the fish and other ingredients, finishing with a layer of vegetables. Fold the foil around it in a neat parcel; the important point is that the juices should not escape during cooking. This preparation is done ahead of time.

On arrival of the guest, put the package into a casserole and leave it to cook in a moderate (350°F, Mark 4) oven for 40 minutes.

Finally, unseal and tip out the contents, juice and all, into the casserole, which is immediately ready to bring to the table.


### Pescado con Acelgas

Majorcan Fish with Wild Spinach

*Serves 2*

*Acelgas* or wild spinach is a common vegetable in the markets of Spain and Majorca. Elsewhere, fresh or frozen leaf spinach may be used instead.

| | |
|---|---|
| 1 lb (½ kilo) cod, bream or hake | 2 potatoes |
| 1 lemon | 2 tomatoes, sliced |
| Salt and pepper | 6 spring onions, chopped |
| 1 lb (½ kilo) *acelgas* or spinach | 1 tablespoon pine kernels |
| | 1 tablespoon raisins |
| | Butter |

Soak the raisins in water for 2 hours. Clean the fish, sprinkle the inside with lemon juice and salt and rub the outside with salt.

Peel and parboil the potatoes, then line a shallow greased baking dish with thin slices. Lay the fish on top. Remove the stalks from the spinach and chop the leaves. Cover the fish with the spinach, tomatoes, spring onions, pine kernels, drained raisins and salt and pepper to taste.

Dot with butter and cook for 30 to 45 minutes in a moderate oven (350°F, Mark 4) until, when tested with a fork, the flesh comes away from the bone of the fish.

### Pescado en Marinado

Cold Spiced Fish

*Serves 2*

| | |
|---|---|
| 1 lb (½ kilo) cod, bream or hake | 3 tablespoons wine vinegar |
| Seasoned flour | 1 teaspoon sugar |
| Olive oil | 2 bay leaves |
| 3 carrots | Salt and black pepper |
| 3 small onions | 12 black olives, stoned and chopped |
| 2 tablespoons parsley, chopped | |

Cut the fish into slices, coat in seasoned flour and fry in olive oil.

Make the sauce: cut the carrots and onions into rounds (reserving a few onion slices), sprinkle with the parsley and cover with boiling water and simmer for 20 minutes. Add the vinegar, sugar, bay leaves and a little salt and ground black pepper, and continue to simmer for another 5 minutes.

Let the sauce cool, then pour it over the fish slices on a flat serving dish.

Garnish with the olives and the reserved onion slices. Serve cold. Accompanied by a tomato salad with French dressing, this makes an excellent summer dish.

### Salmón Empanado

Spiced Grilled Salmon

*Serves 4*

There is excellent salmon and trout fishing in the north of Spain. The trout from the cold streams which flow down from the Pyrenees towards Pamplona, are described in Hemingway's *The Sun Also Rises*. Some of the best salmon come from the River Deva in its precipitous descent to the sea from Potes and the heights of the Picos de Europa, a little known chain of mountains leafy with beech forests and, in spring, carpeted with rare flowers. Along the winding road through the rocky canyon of the Desfiladero de la Hermida the fishermen stand by the verge displaying their catch. The salmon is not cheap, but it is of the best.

| | |
|---|---|
| 4 salmon steaks | 2 oz (50 gm) cooked ham, |
| Salt and pepper | finely diced |
| Juice of 2 lemons | 1 clove garlic, crushed |
| Olive oil | 4 tablespoons parsley, |
| 4 oz (100 gm) fresh | chopped |
| breadcrumbs | |

Clean and wash the salmon steaks, which should be about a finger thick, and marinate them for about 30 minutes with a little salt, pepper, lots of lemon juice and 1 tablespoon olive oil.

Meanwhile, prepare a mixture from the breadcrumbs, ham, garlic and chopped parsley.

Take the salmon steaks out of the marinade and roll them in this mixture until all sides are coated. Put the salmon under a hot grill and cook for about 3 minutes on each side – depending on the thickness of the fish.

If you prefer the salmon less highly spiced and do not like garlic, omit the coating, but marinate it as described, then dot it with butter and grill.

## Sardinas Fritas

Fried Fresh Sardines

| | |
|---|---|
| Fresh sardines | Garlic, crushed |
| 1 egg, beaten | Olive oil |
| Flour or breadcrumbs | |

Clean the sardines, split them from head to tail and remove the backbone. Dip the fish in beaten egg, dredge in flour or breadcrumbs mixed with a crushed clove of garlic and fry in very hot oil.

Alternatively, the sardines may simply be cleaned, dredged with seasoned flour and crisply fried.

They go well with a fresh tomato salad served on the side.

## Vieiras Fritas

Fried Scallops

*Serves 3*

| | |
|---|---|
| 6 scallops | Salt and pepper |
| 2 oz (50 gm) butter | 3 tablespoons parsley, |
| Juice of 1 lemon | chopped |
| Flour | |

Clean the fish and soak in half of the lemon juice for 30 minutes. Remove and coat with the seasoned flour. Heat the butter in a frying-pan until smoking, then reduce the heat and fry the scallops slowly for 5 minutes on each side (or a little longer, depending on their size). Add the rest of the lemon juice and the parsley and serve at once.

### Zarzuela de Pescado a la Catalana

Zarzuela

The Spanish word means a variety show; and a variety of fish in a piquant sauce is just what this dish is. Originating from the Catalan coast, it is now popular all over Spain.

*For each person:*
1 inkfish (squid)
6 mussels

1 large prawn
2 or 3 pieces of firm white
    fish

*For the sauce:* (enough for 2)
1 large onion, finely chopped
Olive oil
2 oz (50 gm) can concentrated
    tomato purée
1 glass white wine
1 small glass brandy

1 pinch saffron
1 clove garlic
5 almonds
1 cream cracker
3 tablespoons parsley,
    chopped

Clean and slice the inkfish (see page 47). Cook the mussels and remove them from their shells (see page 51–2). (As with *paella*, preserved mussels in vinegar are *not* suitable.) Reserve mussel liquor. Fry the onion slowly in a little olive oil for about 15 minutes. Before it browns, add the inkfish, then fry for a further 5 minutes. Transfer to a *cazuela* or casserole and add $\frac{1}{3}$ pint (2 dl) of fish stock (reserved from cooking the mussels). Stir in the wine, brandy and tomato purée.

In the same pan fry the white fish in a little olive oil, then add to the *cazuela* together with the mussels and prawns and simmer for 18 to 20 minutes, taking care that the fish does not disintegrate.

Meanwhile, take a mortar and pound the saffron, garlic, almonds, cream cracker and parsley. Stir in two drops of olive oil to make a paste and add the mixture to the *cazuela*. Serve directly from the *cazuela* or casserole in which you have cooked the fish.

This dish is best prepared in Spain, where it is customary to use a larger variety of the abundant shellfish and to dispense with white fish altogether, except for a small amount of *rape*, which is a firm fish akin to skate.

# 6

# *Meat*

## Albondiguillas en Salsa Española

Meat Balls in Sauce

*Serves 4*

Meat balls in *salsa española* are popular as a *tapa* or appetizer in the bars of Spain and Majorca. They are just as good at home and can also be served with plain boiled potatoes or rice as a supper dish.

| | |
|---|---|
| 2 lb (1 kilo) minced veal and pork, mixed | Salt and pepper |
| 1 tablespoon parsley, chopped | Seasoned flour |
| 1 clove garlic, crushed | Olive oil |
| 1 egg, beaten | 1 pint ($\frac{1}{2}$ litre) *salsa española* (see page 6) |
| 2 oz (50 gm) fresh breadcrumbs | |

Mix the meat, parsley, garlic, egg, breadcrumbs and a little salt and pepper in a bowl. Shape into small meat balls. Dredge with flour and fry crisp in hot olive oil.

On top of the stove, heat up the *salsa española* in a shallow *cazuela* or casserole – which also does duty as a serving dish – and add the meat balls. Simmer in the sauce for 1 hour to 1 hour 30 minutes.

## Bandeja de Fiambres

Assorted Cold Meats

*Chorizo de Pamplona*
*Lomo*
*Jamón Serrano*
*Jamón de York*
} See pages 130–31

Cut the *chorizo* and *lomo* into thin slices – or get the grocer to do it for you – and arrange on a large dish together with slices of the jamón.

Serve with a salad of tomatoes or fresh red or green peppers and French dressing.

### *Cacerola de Chuletas de Cordero*

Casseroled Lamb Chops

*Serves 4*

| | |
|---|---|
| 8 lamb chops or cutlets | Salt and pepper |
| 4 potatoes, sliced | Sprig of rosemary |
| 3 onions, sliced | 1 tablespoon parsley, |
| 8 oz (200 gm) can of tomatoes | chopped |

Place the chops on the bottom of an ovenproof dish and cover with layers of potatoes and onions. Sieve the tomatoes, season with salt and pepper and pour on top of the vegetables. Add the rosemary, cover the dish, put it into a hot oven (400°F, Mark 6), then reduce the heat to moderate (350°F, Mark 4) and cook for 2 hours 30 minutes. Sprinkle with parsley before serving.

### *Callos a la Madrileña*

Tripe Madrid-style

*Serves 4*

| | |
|---|---|
| 2 lb (1 kilo) cleaned boiled tripe | 2 or 3 chunks *chorizo* (see page 131) |
| 1 pig's trotter | 1 clove garlic, crushed |
| 1 red pepper | ½ teaspoon chilli powder |
| 1 onion, chopped | Olive oil |
| 1 tomato, peeled and sliced | Salt |
| 8 oz (200 gm) cooked ham, chopped | |

61

Buy boiled and cleaned tripe and cut it into thin strips. Simmer for 1 hour 30 minutes in salted water, together with the pig's trotter, previously blanched in boiling water and well scraped.

Take out the trotter with a draining spoon, put it on a plate and separate the tender meat from the bones. Return this meat to the saucepan with the tripe.

Remove the seeds from the red pepper, cut it into strips and fry in olive oil with the onion and tomato until soft. Add the ham, garlic, chilli powder and the chunks of *chorizo*. Stir well, then pour the sauce into the stewed tripe – by now the original amount of water will be much reduced – and simmer gently for another 10 to 15 minutes.

### Carne de Vaca Rellena

Majorcan Braised Beef

*Serves 4*

| | |
|---|---|
| 2 lb (1 kilo) braising beef | 1 red pepper |
| Salt and pepper | 8 oz (200 gm) cooked leaf |
| 4 oz (100 gm) olives, stoned | spinach |
| and chopped | 1 clove garlic, crushed |
| 2 hard-boiled eggs, chopped | 1 lemon |

In Majorca this is made with *carne de vaca* (see page 135). Braising beef is as good or better. Buy a thick, flat piece and open it like a book by cutting through the middle of the longest side, so as to leave a 'binding' at the back. Inside the beef, spread salt, freshly ground black pepper, olives, hard-boiled egg, red pepper, spinach, garlic and the juice of a lemon. Close the 'book' and secure the open ends of meat with skewers.

Wrap in foil, place in an ovenproof dish and cook slowly in a moderate oven (350°F, Mark 4) for 2 to 3 hours. Allow to cool, then remove the skewers and cut into thin slices. Serve with a green salad.

### Cerdo Rebozado

Pork in Egg and Breadcrumbs

Ask the butcher for the same cut of pork that you would use for *Wiener schnitzel* in the case of veal and ask him to flatten the meat by smacking it with the side of a chopper. This can be done at home, but not as efficiently, by placing the meat between greaseproof paper and hammering it with a rolling pin.

The pork is cooked exactly as for *Filetes de Ternera Rebozados* (see page 66) and served as described with green peppers. It makes an excellent dish for a dinner party.

### Cochinillo Asado

Roast Sucking Pig

*Serves 8 to 10*

A sucking pig is in fact a piglet which has fed on nothing but milk. Notwithstanding, it is big enough to provide a meal for at least 8 persons and is, for example, an alternative to the Christmas turkey.

In the words of Richard Ford, 'In Spain pigs are more numerous than asses, since they pervade the provinces.' Again, '... the pork of Spain has always been, and is, unequalled in flavour ...' Without being invidious, the best Spanish pork comes from north-west of Madrid. To taste roast sucking pig in perfection, it is well worth while to take the ancient train that rattles down the 50 miles of track to Segovia and to seek out the *Mesón de Cándido*, tucked beneath the Roman aqueduct.

The sucking pig will already have been opened and cleaned by the butcher, and may be roasted either plain or stuffed.

Here is a Spanish recipe for stuffing:

4 oz (100 gm) sausagemeat
8 oz (200 gm) cooked or smoked ham, chopped
The liver from the piglet, chopped
8 oz (200 gm) mushrooms, chopped
6 shallots, chopped
2 eggs, beaten

4 oz (100 gm) fresh breadcrumbs
1 tablespoon parsley, chopped
Salt and pepper
1 teaspoon mixed herbs
1 small glass *aguardiente* (or brandy)
Olive oil

Thoroughly mix all the ingredients together (except the olive oil). Open the piglet, fill the cavity with the stuffing and sew it up with a strong needle and thread. Smear the outside with olive oil and coarse salt and stand on an oven rack in the roasting tin.

If unstuffed, the pig should simply be rubbed with oil and salt, opened and placed on the oven rack. It is also a good idea to put a bit of foil around the mouth and ears to prevent them blackening.

For an 8 to 10 lb ($3\frac{1}{2}$ to $4\frac{1}{2}$ kilo) sucking pig, make sure that the oven is really hot, then roast at a moderate heat (375°F, Mark 5) for 2 hours 15 minutes to 2 hours 45 minutes, with an additional 15 minutes at 425°F, Mark 7, to crisp the outside. In Spain, where ovens are not always efficient, it is often the custom to take the pig to the local bakery for roasting.

Before carving, garnish with an apple in the mouth.

### Cordero Lechazo Asado a la Manchega

Roast Baby Lamb

*Serves 4–6*

In Spain baby milk-fed lamb is delicious; it is cooked to

perfection, succulent and crisp on the outside, in the small restaurants of Logroño and Haro at the Fiesta of San Mateo, beginning on September 21st before the picking of the grapes in Rioja.

The meat does not keep and must be bought very fresh. If the whole lamb is too large for you, the butcher will cut it across the middle with a cleaver.

1 baby lamb
Salt and pepper
1 bay leaf
1 large glass white wine

1 clove garlic
1 tablespoon parsley,
   chopped

*Lechazo* is always roasted. Put it in a roasting tin, season with salt and pepper, then add the bay leaf and most of the white wine. Cook in a hot oven (425°F, Mark 7) for 15 minutes per pound (30 minutes per kilo), basting it occasionally. When cooked, place on a hot serving dish. Add the peeled clove of garlic, chopped parsley and the remaining wine to the juices in the roasting tin. Bring to the boil, remove the bay leaf and pour the sauce over the meat.

Serve with sauté potatoes, fried aubergines (eggplant), or a green salad.

### *Emparedados de Ternera y Jamón*

Fried Veal and Ham Sandwich

1 large escalope of veal per
   person
1 slice cooked ham per
   person

1 egg, beaten
Breadcrumbs
Olive oil
Butter

The veal escalopes must be beaten thin. Cut each in two and place the slice of ham in between, making a sandwich, which is pinned together with the broken halves of a cocktail stick. Coat with egg and breadcrumbs and fry in a mixture of olive oil and butter as described for veal escalopes (see below). Serve with fried green peppers (see page 67).

## Estofado de Cordero

Spanish Lamb Stew

*Serves 4*

| | |
|---|---|
| 2 lb (1 kilo) best end of neck of lamb | 2 glasses dry white wine or sherry |
| Flour | ⅓ pint (scant ¼ litre) water |
| Olive oil | 1 teaspoon mixed dried herbs |
| 1 large onion, sliced | Salt and pepper |

Cut the lamb into small pieces. Dip them in flour and fry in olive oil for 4 to 5 minutes on a high heat. Transfer the meat to a stewpan or *cazuela*.

Add the onion to the same frying pan and oil, fry for 4 to 5 minutes. Drain and add to the meat, together with the sherry or white wine, water, mixed herbs, and a little salt and pepper.

Stew gently for 1 hour or until tender.

## Filetes de Ternera Rebozados con Pimientos Fritos

Veal Escalopes with Fried Sweet Peppers

| | |
|---|---|
| 1 fillet of veal per person | Breadcrumbs |
| 1 green pepper per person | Olive oil |
| Salt and pepper | Butter |
| 1 egg, beaten | |

One of the best and simplest methods of cooking veal is to dip it in beaten egg and breadcrumbs, as for *Wiener schnitzel*, and then fry it in a mixture of olive oil and butter.

Since the veal in Spain is sometimes tougher than elsewhere owing to lack of proper hanging, make sure that the butcher flattens the escalopes (*filetes*) with a chopper, or you can put them between greaseproof paper and tenderize them by flattening them with a rolling pin.

Put equal parts of butter and olive oil into a large frying-pan and get the mixture really hot. Coat the meat with seasoned egg and then breadcrumbs, brown on both sides, then reduce the heat and cook the meat thoroughly. The escalopes are turned occasionally – but not too often, or the breadcrumbs will end up on the bottom of the pan instead of forming a crisp, golden covering. Turn up the heat again for the last few minutes to make sure that the meat is really hot.

The best accompaniment to this dish is whole, fresh green peppers. Begin cooking them about an hour before you want the meal to be ready. Place the whole peppers in a pan with a small quantity of olive oil and cover. Fry the peppers very slowly, turning them several times, replacing the lid to prevent the contents from spluttering.

The peppers are served individually on a side plate and the seeds removed at the table. This is simply done by splitting them from end to end and carrying the knife around the stalk and capsule at the top. The unwanted centre section will come away in one piece, leaving an aromatic juice which goes beautifully with the veal.

### *Greixera de Carne*

Majorcan Beef Stew

*Serves 4*

2 lb (1 kilo) stewing beef or shin of beef
Olive oil
2 onions, chopped
3 tomatoes, peeled and chopped
1 glass red wine
⅓ pint (¼ litre) beef stock or beef stock cube dissolved in water

8 oz (200 gm) peas and/or broad beans
2 oz (50 gm) *chorizo*, sliced
1 teaspoon tarragon, chopped
Salt and pepper

Cut the meat into large pieces and fry in a little olive oil. Transfer to a stew-pan. Fry the onions, add them to the meat, together with the tomatoes, red wine and stock. Stew slowly for 3 hours 30 minutes, if using shin of beef or about 2 hours for stewing beef. Twenty minutes before the dish is ready add the peas and/or beans, *chorizo*, and tarragon. Season to taste.

### *Higado de Ternera Salteado al Vino o Jerez*

Veal Liver Sautéed in Wine or Sherry

*Serves 2*

| | |
|---|---|
| 1 onion, chopped | 1 tablespoon parsley, chopped |
| Butter | Salt and pepper |
| 1 lb (½ kilo) calf's or lambs' liver | 1 glass white wine or sherry |
| 1 tablespoon *salsa española* (see page 6) | |

Fry the chopped onion in butter until almost tender. Cut the liver into thin slices, add, and cook quickly on both sides. While the mixture is still frying, mix in the *salsa española*, parsley, salt, pepper and the white wine or sherry.

### *Higado Rebozado*

Liver in Egg and Breadcrumbs

Large fillets of calf's liver may also be cooked like veal escalopes (see page 66), after dipping in beaten egg and breadcrumbs.

| | |
|---|---|
| 1 large slice calf's liver per person | 1 egg, beaten |
| | Breadcrumbs |

Coat the fillets with egg and breadcrumbs and fry slowly in butter until they are golden on the outside and still pink in the middle. Serve with a few slices of onion fried soft in butter and sauté potatoes.

### Lengua con Salsa de Tomate

Tongue in Tomato Sauce

*Serves 6*

| | |
|---|---|
| 1 ox tongue | $\frac{3}{4}$ pint ($\frac{1}{2}$ litre) *salsa española* |
| 2 onions, sliced | (see page 6) |
| 1½ teaspoons mixed dried | 1 glass sherry |
| herbs | 1 pinch saffron. |
| Salt | |

Buy a large uncooked ox tongue from the butcher. Simmer it with the onions and dried herbs in a large pan of salted water for 3 to 4 hours or until tender. The liquid may be kept for soups. (If salted tongue is used, it must be soaked overnight.)

Once the tongue is cooked, lift it on to a dish and peel off the tough outer skin. Next, roll it into a circular shape and put it in a bowl as nearly as possible the same size, cover it with a flat plate that will sink into the bowl and put a heavy weight on top. If possible, cook and press the tongue a day in advance of eating; it will then be much easier to carve.

Slice the tongue thinly, put the *salsa española* in a fireproof dish. Stir in the sherry and saffron. Add the tongue and simmer gently for about 15 minutes.

This is a good dish for a dinner party since, apart from the final heating, all the work can be done well beforehand. It is best served with plain boiled potatoes.

### *Lengua de Cordero Estallenchs*

Lambs' Tongues in Majorcan Sauce

*Serves 4*

| | |
|---|---|
| 2 lbs (1 kilo) lambs' tongues | Salt and pepper |
| Olive oil or butter | 1 glass white wine |
| 2 onions, finely chopped | Flour |
| 3 tomatoes, peeled and sliced | 16 capers |
| 1 teaspoon mixed dried herbs | 2 oz (50 gm) *chorizo*, thinly |
| 2 tablespoons parsley, | sliced |
| chopped | |

Wash the tongues and blanch in boiling water before removing the tough outer skin. Put them in a pan with the oil or butter, onion, tomatoes, herbs and parsley. Add salt and pepper to taste, the wine and a little water, thicken with the flour, and simmer for 1 hour.

Garnish with the capers and slices of *chorizo* and serve with sauté potatoes.

### *Pierna de Cordero a la Española*

Leg of Lamb

*Serves 4 to 6*

| | |
|---|---|
| Leg of lamb | 1 teaspoon mixed dried herbs |
| 6 shallots | 1 clove garlic, crushed |
| 4 tablespoons parsley, | 1 glass sherry |
| chopped | |

This recipe is also suitable for shoulder of lamb.

Wash the leg of lamb and place in a roasting tin with the peeled shallots around it. Sprinkle the parsley over the lamb. Add the dried herbs, and sherry. Leave to marinate for 2 to 3 hours.

Add a little water to the roasting tin and roast the joint in a moderate oven (350°F, Mark 4) at 15 minutes per pound (40 minutes per kilo) or until tender.

Serve with roast potatoes and a green vegetable or with a green salad and French dressing.

### Pierna de Cordero con Salsa de Granada

Leg of Lamb with Pomegranate Sauce

*Serves 4 to 6*

| | |
|---|---|
| 1 boned leg of lamb | 1 glass dry white wine |
| 12 shallots | 1 pomegranate |

Ask the butcher to bone and tie the leg of lamb. Before roasting, prick all over the top skin with a sharp fork. Put the lamb into a roasting tin surrounded by the shallots and pour the wine over the meat. Cook at 15 minutes per pound (30 minutes per kilo), the first 30 minutes in a hot oven.

Meantime, cut the pomegranate into quarters and scoop out the pips – being careful to remove the bitter white membrane. Add the pomegranate pips and continue cooking in a moderate oven (350°F, Mark 4) for a further 15 minutes.

Carve the meat and serve the pomegranate gravy from the roasting tin separately.

### Riñones a la Broche de Inca

Kidneys on the Spit from Inca

*Serves 4*

| | |
|---|---|
| 2 lb (1 kilo) lambs' kidneys | 1 tablespoon red wine |
| Butter | 1 teaspoon cornflour |
| Flour | 1 clove garlic, crushed |
| Olive oil | Salt and pepper |
| 2 lemons (1 sliced, 1 squeezed) | |

Treat the kidneys as for Kidneys in Sherry (see below), skin and core, cut into pieces and dip in melted butter and flour.

Fry in butter or olive oil, then thread on 4 skewers, separating the pieces of kidney with slices of lemon. Keep hot. Using the same frying-pan, add the red wine and corn-flour and cook gently until the sauce thickens. Add the lemon juice, garlic, and salt and pepper to taste.

Serve the sauce on the side with dishes of boiled rice and fried mushrooms.

### *Riñones al Jerez*

Kidneys in Sherry

*Serves 4*

2 lb (1 kilo) lambs' kidneys
Vinegar
Butter
½ pint (¼ litre) *salsa española*
  (see page 6)

2 glasses dry sherry
1 clove garlic, crushed

Wash the kidneys and soak for an hour in cold water and vinegar. Drain and rinse, remove skin and membranes, and cut into slices with scissors. Fry for 5 minutes in salted butter, turning them from time to time. Have ready a *cazuela* or casserole containing the *salsa española*. Add the kidneys, sherry and garlic and stew very slowly for 1 hour.

Serve with fresh bread to dunk in the sauce.

### *Riñones con Salsa Mibar*

Kidneys Mibar

*Serves 4*

| 2 lb (1 kilo) lambs' kidneys | 2 glasses dry sherry |
| 2 onions, chopped | 1 clove garlic, crushed |
| Olive oil or butter | Salt and pepper |
| 1 teaspoon flour | 2 hard-boiled eggs, chopped |

Treat the kidneys as for Kidneys in Sherry (see page 72). Skin, core and cut them into thin slices.

Fry the onions in butter or olive oil until golden. Add the kidney slices, continue frying for some minutes, then stir in a teaspoon of flour, the sherry and garlic, season to taste, and simmer for 30 minutes, or until tender. Add the chopped eggs just before serving.

### *Riñones Salteados Magdalena*

Sautéed Kidneys and Potatoes

*Serves 4*

| 2 lb (1 kilo) sheep's kidneys | Salt and pepper |
| 1 onion, finely chopped | 1 glass white wine or sherry |
| 2 cloves garlic, crushed | 3 boiled potatoes, sliced |
| 1 tablespoon parsley, chopped | Olive oil |

Treat the kidneys as for Kidneys in Sherry (see page 72), then cut into thin slices and put them on a plate with the onion, garlic, chopped parsley, salt and pepper to taste and the white wine or sherry. Mix well together.

Sauté the potatoes in olive oil. When golden, place them on a shallow fireproof dish, covering the surface evenly. Keep warm in the oven.

Using the same pan, fry the kidney mixture for 10 minutes turning once, and then pour it on top of the sauté potatoes.

Cook in a moderate oven (350°F, Mark 4) for 30 minutes.

### Sesos a la Romana

Crisp Fried Brains

*Serves 2*

| | |
|---|---|
| 2 sheeps' brains | Flour |
| Vinegar | Olive oil |
| Salt and pepper | 1 lemon, sliced |
| 2 bay leaves | 1 tablespoon parsley, |
| ½ teaspoon thyme |    chopped |
| 1 egg, beaten | |

Soak the brains for 20 minutes in water and vinegar. Remove the skin and membranes and put them into a pan with water, salt and pepper, bay leaves and thyme. Simmer slowly for 15 minutes.

Throw away the water and cut the brains into small pieces. When cool, roll in egg and flour and fry in hot olive oil until golden. Garnish with lemon slices and parsley.

### Ternera Estofada

Veal Stew

*Serves 4*

Cut up 3 lb (1½ kilo) of shoulder veal, then proceed as for *Pollo a la Vasca* (see page 81). Add ¼ pint (150 ml or 1½ dl) water to the mixture to make more juice.

# Poultry and Game

### *Conejo a la Vinagreta*

Rabbit Vinaigrette

*Serves 4*

| | |
|---|---|
| 1 young rabbit, jointed | 4 onions |
| $\frac{1}{4}$ pint ($1\frac{1}{2}$ dl) vinegar | 12 olives, stoned |
| $\frac{1}{4}$ pint ($1\frac{1}{2}$ dl) olive oil | 1 tablespoon capers |
| $\frac{1}{4}$ pint ($1\frac{1}{2}$ dl) water | 1 tablespoon gherkins |
| Salt and pepper | 2 sprigs parsley |
| 1 clove garlic | |

Put the rabbit into a deep greased casserole with the vinegar, olive oil, water, salt and pepper to taste, garlic and the onions opened in the shape of a cross.

Grill the rabbit's liver and mince with the olives, capers, gherkins and parsley. Add to the casserole and stew the contents gently for about an hour or until tender. If the stew tends to become dry, it may be necessary to add a little more water.


### *Conejo con Cebolla*

Rabbit with Onions

*Serves 4*

| | |
|---|---|
| 1 young rabbit | Salt and pepper |
| Olive oil | 1 glass sherry or white wine |
| Butter | 4 oz (100 gm) cooked |
| 2 onions, sliced | peas or 1 can small petits |
| 2 or 3 rashers of bacon | pois |

Cut the rabbit into small pieces and fry in a mixture of oil and butter with the onions, bacon, and salt and pepper to taste. When browned, add the sherry or white wine and a little water. Simmer the mixture for an hour or until tender, then add the peas just before serving.

## Conejo con Salsa

Rabbit Supreme

*Serves 4*

4 rashers streaky bacon, without rinds and chopped
Olive oil
1 young rabbit, jointed
Seasoned flour
2 onions, chopped
4 oz (100 gm) lean gammon, diced

4 oz (100 gm) *chorizo*, thinly sliced
2 tablespoons parsley, chopped
1 glass red wine
Salt and pepper

Fry the chopped bacon in a large pan. Remove. Coat the rabbit in seasoned flour, fry in the bacon fat and transfer to an oven dish with the fried bacon.

In the same pan, fry the onions until tender and then add the diced gammon and *chorizo*. Continue frying briefly. Sprinkle with the parsley and stir in the red wine, a glass of water, and season to taste.

Pour this sauce over the rabbit and cook in a moderate oven (350°F, Mark 4) for about an hour or until tender.

Serve with a green vegetable.

## Escaldums de Gallina

Majorcan Stewed Chicken

*Serves 4*

1 boiling fowl
Olive oil
1 onion, chopped
1 clove garlic, crushed
1 tomato, sliced

1 bay leaf
1 glass white wine or vermouth
Slices of *sobreasada* (see page 132)

Steam the chicken for about three hours, depending on the

77

size of the bird. Cut it into pieces and fry in olive oil with the onion. When the chicken and onion have browned, add the garlic and tomato. Stir well, add the bay leaf, wine, and the slices of *sobreasada*, which will dissolve into the stew, giving it a rich red colour.

## Menudillos

Small Fry of Chicken

*Serves 4*

In Spain, many housewives buy chicken pieces rather than the whole bird. The *menudillos*, meaning the giblets, livers and heart, removed during the cleaning, are sold separately. When fried, they make an appetising starter and with the addition of *salsa española* can be served as a light lunch.

| | |
|---|---|
| 2 lb (1 kilo) *menudillos* | 2 hard-boiled eggs, |
| Salt and pepper | chopped |
| 2 tablespoons olive oil | Mustard |
| 1 small onion, chopped | 3 tablespoons *salsa española* |
| 2 cloves garlic, sliced | (see page 6) |
| 4 tablespoons parsley, | |
| chopped | |

Separate the necks from the rest of the *menudillos* and boil in water with salt and pepper to make a chicken broth. Thoroughly wash and clean the hearts and livers, cut them into pieces with a pair of scissors and put aside on a plate.

Heat the olive oil in a frying-pan. Add the onion and fry it gently with the garlic until half-cooked. Add the *menudillos*, chopped parsley, hard-boiled eggs and a little mustard, and continue frying slowly for about 15 minutes.

Stir a little of the chicken broth into the *salsa española*, add and cook for a further 10 minutes.

# Pato Asado con Naranja

Roast Duck with Orange

*Serves 4*

| | |
|---|---|
| 1 duck (4 to 5 lb or 2 kilo) | ½ oz (15 gm) butter |
| ½ teaspoon mixed dried herbs | 1 oz (25 gm) flour |
| Salt and pepper | 2 oranges |

Prick the entire skin of the bird with a fork. This is important since it allows the interior layer of fat to drain away during roasting and the duck, when cooked, will be golden brown and not excessively rich.

Simmer the giblets in 1 pint (½ litre) water with the dried herbs and a little salt, until tender and reduced by half.

Put the duck on an oven rack placed inside the roasting tin, and roast in a hot oven (425°F, Mark 7), for 45 minutes per pound, turning it during cooking.

Meanwhile, make a sauce with the butter, flour, the cooked and seasoned broth from the giblets, and the grated peel and juice from one orange.

Serve this sauce on the side with a dish of green peas and arrange slices from the other orange around the bird.


# Pavo o Capón Mallorquin

Majorcan Stuffed Turkey or Capon

*Serves 4 to 6*

| | |
|---|---|
| 1 turkey or capon | 2 oz (50 gm) raisins |
| 1 chicken stock cube | 4 oz (100 gm) pine kernels |
| 8 oz (200 gm) bacon, diced | 1 glass sherry |
| 4 oz (100 gm) black cherries, stoned | 4 potatoes, parboiled |
| 1 apple, cored and chopped | 4 oz (100 gm) salted butter |
| | 1 clove garlic, crushed |

Simmer the giblets in water with the chicken stock cube to make a rich gravy.

Prepare the stuffing by putting into a bowl the bacon, stoned black cherries, chopped apple, raisins and pine kernels. Mix well with a glass of sherry. Stuff and seal the bird, put in a roasting tin and surround it with the parboiled potatoes.

Melt the butter in a pan. Add the garlic, stir well, and pour over the bird.

Cook for 20 minutes per pound (40 minutes per kilo) in a hot oven (425°F, Mark 7), basting occasionally.

### *Perdices Estofadas a la Castellana*

Stewed Partridge Castilian Style

*Serves 2*

| | |
|---|---|
| 2 partridges | 1 large glass white wine |
| 2 tablespoons olive oil | Salt and pepper |
| 4 oz (100 gm) streaky bacon | |

Clean the partridges, put them into a stew-pan with the oil and fry for 2 minutes. Reduce the heat and add the bacon, white wine and a pinch of salt and pepper. Stew for about 1 hour or until tender.

### *Pollitos Pequeños Fritos*

Fried Spring Chicken

*Serves 2*

Ask the butcher to cut up a small chicken for you.

Dredge the pieces in seasoned flour and fry them crisp in olive oil.

Serve with fried potatoes.

## Pollo a la Vasca

Basque Chicken

*Serves 4*

2 onions, chopped
2 tomatoes, peeled and sliced
3 canned red peppers, cut in
  strips

Olive oil
Salt and pepper
4 chicken joints
Flour

Fry together the onions, tomatoes and red peppers in a little olive oil. Season to taste. Cook slowly until soft, but do not blend or mash.

Meanwhile, coat pieces of chicken with seasoned flour and fry quickly in olive oil. When the chicken is brown on both sides, put it into the sauce already prepared and simmer gently for about 1 hour.

## Pollo en Pepitoria

Chicken with Almonds

*Serves 4*

1 chicken, or equivalent in
  chicken pieces
Seasoned flour
Olive oil
2 onions, chopped
2 glasses white wine

$\frac{1}{2}$ pint ($\frac{1}{4}$ litre) chicken stock
Yolk of 1 hard-boiled egg,
  chopped
12 almonds, blanched and
  chopped
$\frac{1}{2}$ teaspoon mixed dried herbs

Cut up the chicken, dip the pieces in seasoned flour, fry in olive oil and transfer to a stew-pan. Fry the chopped onions and add to the chicken. Pour in the white wine and chicken stock and simmer gently for about 1 hour 30 minutes.

Ten minutes before the dish is ready, add the egg yolk, almonds and dried herbs.

Serve with saffron-flavoured rice.

# 8
# Vegetables

## Alcachofas Cocidas

### Globe Artichokes

Plentiful and cheap in Spain, these are a favourite starter.

| | |
|---|---|
| Globe artichokes | 1 teaspoon flour |
| Juice of 1 lemon | |

The artichokes must be firm. Cut off the stems, remove the outer leaves and trim the points of the others with scissors. Rub over with a slice of lemon to avoid subsequent blackening and boil in salted water with the lemon juice and flour. Do not overcook. When they are ready, the flesh base will 'give' a little if pressed with a fork.

Cool in cold water and serve with French dressing (see page 9) on the side. The artichokes are eaten by first stripping the leaves and sucking the fleshy bases, and then scooping out the heart of the plant with a spoon.

## Berenjenas Catalina

### Aubergine Moulds

*Serves 4*

| | |
|---|---|
| 4 aubergines (eggplants) | 2 onions, chopped |
| Salt and pepper | 4 tomatoes, peeled and sliced |
| 1 red pepper, deseeded and sliced | 4 oz (100 gm) cooked ham, chopped |
| 1 tablespoon parsley, chopped | 4 oz (100 gm) mushrooms, sliced |
| 2 tablespoons olive oil | 1 glass white wine |
| 2 eggs, beaten | |

Peel the aubergines, cut them into strips and soak in cold, salted water for 30 minutes, first removing any large pips. Dry the strips on kitchen paper. Add them to the red pepper

84

and parsley and fry in olive oil on a low heat for 30 minutes. Take the pan off the heat and stir in the eggs.

Pour the mixture into a greased mould, stand it in a tin of water, and bake in the oven for 15 minutes.

To make the sauce, fry the onions until tender. Add the tomatoes, chopped ham, mushrooms and white wine. Simmer gently until cooked. When the mould has set, remove from the oven, turn it out on to a serving dish and pour the sauce around it in a circle.

### *Berenjenas Empanadas de Chorizo*

Aubergine a la Maria Teresa

*Serves 4*

Simple to prepare and economical in Spain – since it combines two of the country's most plentiful ingredients, *chorizo* (see page 131) and the glossy purple aubergine (or eggplant).

Cooked ham may be substituted for *chorizo*.

| | |
|---|---|
| 4 aubergines (eggplants) | ½ teaspoon vinegar |
| 4 oz (100 gm) *chorizo*, thinly sliced | 1 egg, beaten |
| | Salt |
| 2 tablespoons flour | Olive oil |
| 1 tablespoon water | |

Peel the aubergines and then cut them into thin rounds and soak in a bowl of salted water for an hour.

Make a batter with the flour, water, vinegar, egg and a little salt. Sandwich the *chorizo* slices between the rounds of aubergine. Repeat until all the aubergine has been used. Coat the sandwiches with the batter and fry in hot olive oil.

### Berenjenas Rellenas

Stuffed Aubergines

*Serves 2*

2 aubergines (eggplants)
1 onion
Olive oil
2 oz (50 gm) mushrooms, chopped
4 oz (100 gm) minced ham or other meat

1 slice bread, soaked in milk
Salt and pepper
1 tomato, sliced
Butter
2 teaspoons parsley, chopped
2 oz (50 gm) cheese, grated

Cut the aubergines in half lengthways. Soak them in salted water for 30 minutes, removing any large pips. Then, with a sharp knife, cut the pulp out of the halved aubergines, taking care not to damage the shells. Arrange the shells close together in a flat well-greased oven dish.

Mince the aubergine pulp with the onion and fry in olive oil until tender. Add the chopped mushrooms and minced ham, together with the bread. Season well with salt and pepper and mix together. Fill the aubergine halves with this mixture, cover with tomato slices and butter, and sprinkle with the parsley and grated cheese. Cook in a moderate oven (350°F, Mark 4) for 45 minutes.

### Cachelos con Jamón

Red Potatoes with Boiled Ham

*Serves 4*

This spicy dish comes from the Guadarrama Mountains.

2 lb (1 kilo) potatoes
2 tablespoons olive oil

2 cloves garlic, chopped
2 teaspoons paprika

Peel and boil the potatoes. While they are cooking, put the

olive oil into a frying-pan. Add the garlic and fry until brown, being careful not to burn it. Remove from the heat and stir in the paprika. Drain the potatoes and pour the mixture over them while they are still piping hot. Keep on a low heat for a few minutes, shaking the pan, when the potatoes will turn a deep red.

With boiled ham this makes a dish about as warming as neat whisky.

## Calabacines Fritos

Fried Courgettes

*Serves 4*

| | |
|---|---|
| 2 lb (1 kilo) courgettes (baby marrows) | 2 oz (50 gm) butter |

Peel, cut in half lengthways and boil courgettes for 5 minutes. Strain, dry and fry in butter until golden brown.

## Caviar de Berenjenas

Aubergine 'Caviare'

*Serves 2*

| | |
|---|---|
| 2 large aubergines (eggplants) | 1 tablespoon tomato purée |
| 1 tablespoon olive oil | 1 teaspoon wine vinegar |
| 1 onion, chopped | Salt and black pepper |

Peel, slice and soak the aubergines. Fry with the onion for 20 minutes. Drain off the excess oil, and pass the mixture through a sieve or blender. Add the tomato purée, wine vinegar, salt and ground black pepper to taste, and beat with a fork until smooth.

Leave in a dish until cool and serve with squares of toast or biscuits.

## Champiñón (o setas) con Ajo y Perejil

Mushrooms with Garlic and Parsley

*Serves 4*

1 lb (½ kilo) mushrooms
2 oz (50 gm) butter
2 cloves garlic, crushed

3 tablespoons parsley,
  chopped
Salt and pepper

Fry the mushrooms gently in the butter. Add the garlic, chopped parsley and season to taste. Serve hot.

## Coliflor Frita

Fried Cauliflower

*Serves 4*

1 cauliflower
Salt
1 egg, beaten

Seasoned flour
Olive oil

Wash the cauliflower and boil it in salted water for 20 minutes. Drain and cut into pieces. Dip in beaten egg, coat in flour and fry in hot oil.

## Ensalada de Pimientos Rojos

Red Pepper Salad

2 fresh red peppers per person
Olive oil

French dressing (see page 9)

Put the peppers into a frying-pan with a minute amount of olive oil, cover, and fry very slowly for an hour, turning them at intervals. Skin them, remove and discard the seeds and capsules. Cut the peppers into strips and cover with a little French dressing.

### Ensaladilla Rusa

Russian Salad

*Serves 4*

1 lb ($\frac{1}{2}$ kilo) fresh prawns or
  8 oz frozen prawns
1 lb ($\frac{1}{2}$ kilo) potatoes
2 carrots
4 oz (100 gm) peas, shelled
  or frozen

1 can tuna in oil, chopped
$\frac{1}{2}$ pint ($\frac{1}{4}$ litre) *mahonesa muselina* (see page 8)
Few asparagus tips, canned

If the prawns are fresh they must first be boiled and shelled, the stock being kept for soup; frozen prawns are simply thawed.

Boil the vegetables, drain and cool before dicing the potatoes and carrots. Mix in a large bowl with the drained, chopped fish and fluffy mayonnaise. The asparagus may either be served separately or arranged on top of the salad.

### Esparragos

Asparagus

Traditionally, the best asparagus in Spain – though Logroño and the Rioja might well dispute the claim – comes from Aranjuez, a hot and dusty place not far south of Madrid, which has given its name to a rightly famous guitar concerto and also boasts a vast and deserted royal palace.

In Spain, this asparagus is available in cans, but it may also, of course, be cooked fresh. Avoid asparagus with a yellowish appearance, which indicates that it is not entirely fresh. Peel, wash, and cut the stems to the same length, then tie into bundles, making sure that the heads lie in the same direction.

Boil in lightly salted water for eighteen minutes, if the asparagus is thin, or for a few minutes more, if it is thick. Check the progress of cooking by pricking the asparagus with a pin – it is important not to overcook or some of the flavour will be lost.

Drain, remove the string, and turn into a heated dish wrapped in a napkin. Asparagus, either fresh or canned, may be accompanied by mayonnaise (see page 7), vinaigrette sauce (see page 9) or melted butter. A favourite method of serving it with the *Madrileños,* who at summer weekends crowd the restaurants of Aranjuez overlooking the lazy Manzanares river, is in *Ensaladilla Rusa* (see page 89).

## *Pimientos Rellenos*

Stuffed Peppers

*Serves 3*

It is often thought that fresh peppers are required for this dish. But, with care it can be made with the canned variety, and the results are just as good.

| | |
|---|---|
| 4 oz (100 gm) rice | 1 clove garlic, crushed |
| 8 oz (200 gm) frozen shrimps | 1 large can red peppers |
| 6 tomatoes, peeled and chopped | ½ pint (¼ litre) *salsa española* (see page 6) |
| Salt and pepper | |

Boil the rice for 20 minutes, drain and add a mixture of shrimps, tomatoes, salt and pepper and a little crushed garlic.

Empty the peppers into a bowl – each can holds about six. Take out each one carefully, holding it in the palm of the hand while stuffing it with the mixture, so that it does not fall apart. Secure at each end with a toothpick, then lay the stuffed peppers in a *cazuela* or casserole just big enough to take them comfortably.

Pour the *salsa española* over the peppers. Cook on top of the stove for about 30 minutes covering with a lid to retain the aromatic vapour.


### Pimientos Rojos con Carne

Red Peppers with Meat

*Serves 3*

Red peppers go well with veal escalopes or fillets or pork cooked the same way as *Wiener schnitzel* (see page 66) and are a pleasant change.

| | |
|---|---|
| Olive oil | 1 large can red peppers |
| 2 cloves garlic, chopped | Salt |

Heat a little olive oil and fry the garlic, being careful not to let it burn, as this can happen very easily. Cut the peppers into narrow strips, and when the garlic is beginning to brown, add them to the pan, cover with a lid, and continue cooking over a low heat for about 30 minutes. Add a little salt.

Preheat some small *cazuelas* or individual casseroles in the oven and serve the peppers as a side dish.


### Pisto

*Serves 4*

This is a Spanish version of the French *ratatouille*, often served with roast veal or lamb. Alternatively, it can be eaten as a dish on its own, with eggs broken into it as cooking finishes.

Olive oil
1 large onion, sliced
1 lb (½ kilo) courgettes
  (baby marrows)
1 lb (½ kilo) green peppers
1 lb (½ kilo) fresh or canned
  tomatoes

1 potato
1 clove garlic, crushed
Salt
1 egg per person (optional)

Put a small amount of olive oil into a large *cazuela* or stew-pan and fry the onion slowly for 3 to 4 minutes. Remove the seeds from the peppers, cut into small pieces and add. Next add the peeled and sliced potato, cooking for another 2 or 3 minutes before addition of the courgettes, washed and cut into small rounds.

Drain off all excess oil and stir in the tomatoes, which will provide sufficient liquid for further cooking. Season with the garlic and a little salt. Simmer slowly for about 1 hour 30 minutes.

### Tomates a la Jardinera

Stuffed Tomatoes

*Serves 6*

12 tomatoes
4 oz (100 gm) green
  beans, fresh or frozen
4 oz (100 gm) peas, shelled
  or frozen

Few small artichoke hearts,
  canned
Few asparagus tips, canned
Mayonnaise (see page 7)

Scoop out the centres of the tomatoes and keep for soup. Cook the beans and peas. Chop small with the artichoke hearts and asparagus tips and add some thick mayonnaise.

Fill the tomatoes with the mixture and cool in the refrigerator for 2 hours before serving.

*Tumbet*

*Serves 4*

There is no translation for this dish. It is as typical of Majorca as is *moussaka*, which it resembles, of Greece.

| | |
|---|---|
| 8 oz (200 gm) aubergines | 8 oz (200 gm) minced beef |
| 8 oz (200 gm) potatoes | 2 onions, sliced |
| Olive oil | 1 pint (½ litre) *salsa española* |
| 8 oz (200 gm) red peppers | (see page 6) |

Cut the aubergines and soak in salted water for 30 minutes. Fry separately in hot oil, rounds of peeled parboiled potatoes, the peppers, beef, the dried rounds of aubergine and onions. Keep on separate plates. Into a large ovenproof dish, put layers of the fried ingredients, spreading *salsa española* over the top of each.

Cook in a moderate oven (350°F, Mark 4) for an hour.

# 9

# Mixed Dishes

## Canalones a la Rossini

Cannelloni a la Rossini

*Serves 6*

A virtue of these Spanish-style *cannelloni* is that the pasta
bought ready-made in wafers, is excessively thin, forming
little more than an envelope to enclose the savoury filling.
This pasta, which requires no cooking but only soaking in
cold water, is available in boxes of 12 or 18 pieces at any
Spanish grocer or good delicatessen.

1 onion, chopped
Olive oil
2 lb (1 kilo) minced pork
  and veal, chicken livers and
  bacon or ham
Salt
1 brain (cook as on page 74)
Fresh breadcrumbs
1 egg
1 glass sherry
1 tablespoon parsley,
  chopped

1 pint ($\frac{1}{2}$ litre) *salsa española*
  (see page 6)
Nutmeg
1 small tin of inexpensive
  liver pâté
1 pint ($\frac{1}{2}$ litre) white sauce
  (see page 5)
4 oz (100 gm) cheese, grated
3 oz (75 gm) butter
24–30 cannelloni squares of
  pasta

Fry the onion in a little olive oil for 10 minutes. Add the
pork and veal, chicken livers and bacon or ham, all minced
and mixed, and fry for another 10 minutes, adding salt.
Meanwhile prepare the brain, washing and cooking it as
described on page 74, and put it on a plate.

Now mince the mixture of meat and onion into a large
bowl. Stir in sufficient breadcrumbs to thicken it, and then
add the egg, sherry, chopped parsley, three tablespoons
*salsa española* and a little ground nutmeg. Continue stirring
with the addition of the cooked brain and pâté.

This completes the preparation of the filling, which may
be kept in the refrigerator, until the next day if necessary, to
await filling into the cannelloni.

Immerse the wafers of pasta in cold water, using a large
bowl or saucepan to avoid their sticking together. It is

better to soak them for 2 hours, rather than 1 as recommended in the instructions. Place a clean kitchen cloth on the table and lay out the squares of pasta in rows. Dry carefully by blotting with another cloth.

With a spoon, put a dollop of the filling at the centre of each square, and roll the pasta around the filling to form tubes.

Pour half the white sauce, made with the addition of half the grated cheese, into the bottom of a large oven dish and on top of this lay out the cannelloni in rows, each being separated from the row above by a layer of cheese, sauce and *salsa española*.

Decorate with a little of the *salsa española* poured in a thin cord between the cannelloni. Dot with knobs of butter and sprinkle the remaining grated cheese over the surface.

All this may be done well in advance of cooking, for which an hour is required in a slow oven (325°F, Mark 3).

Served with a green salad and followed by fresh fruit, these cannelloni make a veritable feast.


### Delicias de Queso

Cheese Savouries

| | |
|---|---|
| 6 egg whites | Cayenne pepper |
| 8 oz (200 gm) grated | 2 eggs, beaten |
|   Gruyère cheese | Fresh breadcrumbs |
| White pepper | Olive oil |

Whisk the egg whites until stiff, mix with the grated cheese and season with white and cayenne pepper. Shape into balls or croquettes between two spoons. Dip in beaten egg and breadcrumbs and fry crisp in hot oil until golden. Serve very hot.

### Delicias de Queso y Jamón

Cheese and Ham Savouries

Proceed exactly as for the *Delicias de Queso*, but use half cheese and half cooked ham, chopped or minced. Alternatively, all of the cheese may be replaced by ham.

### Delicias de Almendras

Yet another variation, suitable for a dessert, is made with grated almonds. In this case the cayenne pepper is omitted.

### Fabada Asturiana

*Serves 6*

One of the most famous dishes of northern Spain.

2 pig's trotters
1 lb (½ kilo) fresh brisket of beef, cut in cubes
2 lb (1 kilo) dry butter beans
8 oz (200 gm) *chorizo*

8 oz (200 gm) *morcilla asturiana* or black pudding (see page 131)
1 large onion, quartered
Salt and pepper

First wash and blanch the pig's trotters, then put them into a large saucepan with the brisket, the quartered onion and the butter beans. Cover with water, bring to the boil, skim with a spoon and then reduce the heat, simmering slowly for about 2 to 3 hours until the meat and beans are tender. Add the *chorizo* and *morcilla* in chunks 30 minutes before the dish is ready, and season to taste.

## Fritos de Queso

Cheese Fritters

*Serves 3*

1 egg
1 box Brie or ½ box Camem-
   bert (or other soft cheese)

1 dessertspoon made English
   mustard
Pinch of cayenne pepper
Breadcrumbs
Olive oil

First cut the cheese into small triangles and dip them into a paste made from the mustard and cayenne pepper. Coat with fine breadcrumbs, then with beaten egg and again with breadcrumbs. Fry in very hot oil.

These fritters can be made with any creamy cheese – as long as it is not runny.


## Olla Podrida

To describe this national dish of Spain, we cannot do better than quote from the inimitable *Gatherings From Spain*, written in 1846 by Richard Ford, who was as good a cook as an acute observer of life and manners.

'Into this *olla* it may be affirmed that the whole culinary genius of Spain is condensed, as the mighty Jinn was into a gallipot, according to the Arabian Night tales. The lively gastronomic French, who are decidedly the leaders of European civilization in the kitchen, deride the barbarous practices of the Gotho-Iberians, as being darker than Erebus and more ascetic than aesthetic; to credit their authors, a Peninsular breakfast consists of a teaspoonful of chocolate, a dinner, of a knob of garlic soaked in water, and a supper, of a paper cigarette; and according to their *parfait cuisinier*, the *olla* is made of two cigars boiled in three gallons of water – but this is a calumny, a mere invention devised by the enemy . . .

'. . . the cook must throw his whole soul into the pan, or

99

rather pot; it may be made in one, but two are better. They must be earthenware; for, like the French *pot au feu*, the dish is good for nothing when made in an iron or copper vessel.

'Place into No. 1 [pot] *Garbanzos* [(see page 102)], which have been placed to soak over-night. Add a good piece of beef, a chicken, a large piece of bacon; let it boil once and quickly; then let it simmer; it requires four or five hours to be well done. Meanwhile place into No. 2, with water, whatever vegetables are to be had: lettuces, cabbage, a slice of gourd, of beet, carrots, beans, celery, endive, onions and garlic, long peppers. These must be previously well washed and cut, as if they were destined to make a salad; then add red sausages, or *chorizos*; half a salted pig's face, which should have been soaked over-night. When all is sufficiently boiled, strain off the water, and throw it away. Remember constantly to skim the scum off both saucepans. When all this is sufficiently dressed, take a large dish, lay in the bottom the vegetables, the beef in the centre, flanked by the bacon, chicken, and pig's face. The sausages should be arranged around, *en couronne*; pour over some of the soup from No. 1, and serve hot . . .

'This is the *olla en grande*, such as Don Quixote says was only eaten by canons and presidents of colleges. . . . In fact, as a general rule, anything that is good in itself is good for an *olla*, provided, as old Spanish books always conclude, that it contains nothing contrary to the holy mother church, to orthodoxy, and to good manners . . . Of course, every *olla* must everywhere be made according to what can be got. In private families the contents of No. 1, the soup, is served up with bread, in a tureen, and the frugal table decked with the separate contents of the *olla* in separate platters; the remains coldly served, or are warmed up, for supper.

'The vegetables and bacon are absolute necessaries; without the former an *olla* has neither grace nor sustenance; *la olla sin verdura, ni tiene gracia ni hartura*, while the latter is as essential in this stew as a text from St. Augustine is in a sermon . . .'

## *Pan de Ajo*

Garlic Bread

1 French loaf                           3 cloves garlic, crushed
3 oz (75 gm) butter

Cut the loaf in thick slices, nearly all the way through but not quite, so that it still holds together. Melt the butter in a saucepan and when it begins to bubble add the garlic. Stir and remove from the heat before it browns. Pour the mixture slowly into the cuts, then put the loaf in a hot oven for about 10 minutes until crisp on the outside.

Serve piping hot – and heaven help your waistline!


## *Perlas Negras*

Black Pearls

This attractive aperitif is made in Spain with the inexpensive and readily available foie gras; truffles, too, are not unduly expensive. In most other places it would be a luxury dish.

8 oz (200 gm) foie gras              3 truffles
3 oz (75 gm) butter                 Sprig parsley
2 tablespoons dry sherry

Mix the foie gras and butter, smooth through a sieve and add a little salt, pepper and the sherry. Put in the refrigerator to let it harden. Meanwhile chop the truffles as fine as you can.

From the mixture, which must be very cold, now shape small balls about the size of hazelnuts and coat them with the chopped truffle. Garnish with parsley and serve in a decorative glass dish.

### Potaje de Garbanzos
Chickpea Potage
*Serves 4*

This is a meal in itself, popular in the mountainous north of
Spain, and particularly warming in the English winter. The
same recipe is equally suitable for dry kidney beans or
lentils. A somewhat similar dish made with butter beans is
known as *Fabada Asturiana* (see page 98).

| | |
|---|---|
| 8 oz (200 gm) chickpeas | 1 pig's trotter |
| 1 large onion, chopped | 4 oz (100 gm) *chorizo* and/or |
| 2 or 3 bay leaves | black pudding |
| 2 cloves garlic, crushed | Salt and pepper |
| 1 teaspoon mixed dried herbs | |

Soak the dried chickpeas overnight, by which time they will
soften and absorb most of the water.

Next day put them in a large stew-pan with boiling water,
the onion, bay leaves, garlic, the mixed dried herbs – or
even better, fresh mint – and the pig's trotter, scraped clean
and blanched in boiling water. Bring back to the boil and
simmer for about 2 hours 30 minutes or until tender. Thirty
minutes before the potage is ready, add several chunks of
*chorizo* and/or black pudding and salt and pepper to taste.

### Sandwich Caliente
Toasted Sandwich
*Serves 2*

This is a popular snack in the Madrid cafeterias. At home,
it makes an appetizing light lunch or supper.

| | |
|---|---|
| 3 oz (75 gm) butter | 2 thin slices Cheddar or |
| 4 thin slices of bread | *Manchego* cheese |
| 2 hard-boiled eggs, sliced | 2 tomatoes, peeled and sliced |
| 6 rashers green bacon or 2 | 4 lettuce leaves |
| thin rounds *Jamón de York*, | |
| grilled | |

Melt the butter either on a griddle, such as the Scots use for making pancakes, or on the hot plate of an electric cooker. If you have neither of these, you can make do with a heavy frying-pan. Cut the crusts from the bread and brown on a gentle heat.

Meanwhile, have ready the hard-boiled eggs, the ham or grilled rashers of bacon, the slices of cheese, the sliced tomatoes and a few lettuce leaves.

When brown on one side, turn all the bread over and put more butter on the griddle. On two of the slices, place first the cheese, giving it time to melt a little, then the grilled bacon, the lettuce, the rounds of hard-boiled egg and finally the tomatoes. Increase the heat as all four slices brown on the second side.

Cover the sandwiches with the second slices of bread, cut in two and serve immediately.

# 10
# Desserts

## Almendrados de Castellón

Almond Macaroons

| | |
|---|---|
| 1 oz (25 gm) almonds | 2 teaspoons powdered |
| 2 egg whites | cinnamon |
| 1 oz (25 gm) caster sugar | Grated lemon peel |
| Salt | |

Blanch and chop the almonds. Beat the egg whites stiff in a bowl with a little of the sugar and a pinch of salt, then mix in the rest of the sugar, the cinnamon and lemon peel.

Spoon the mixture into small moulds and bake in a moderately hot oven (375°F, Mark 5) until they start to turn brown.

## Flan de Huevos

Baked Caramel Custard

*Serves 4*

This is the 'flan' so popular the length and breadth of France and Spain as a dessert.

| | |
|---|---|
| 4 heaped tablespoons caster | 4 large eggs |
| sugar | Salt |
| 1 pint (½ litre) milk | |

The sugar should preferably be flavoured by keeping it in a tin with vanilla pods; otherwise, a little vanilla essence may be used.

Put 3 heaped tablespoons sugar into a pan with 1 teaspoon water and heat until caramelized. Coat the bottom of the flan dish or heatproof pudding bowl with this.

Bring the milk slowly to the boil in another saucepan.

Meanwhile, beat the eggs in a bowl, adding a pinch of salt and the remaining sugar. Once the milk is on the boil, pour it over the egg mixture, stir well and transfer to the caramel-coated flan dish. Stand in water and cook in a moderate oven (350°F, Mark 4) for about an hour until set.

The progress of cooking can be checked by pushing a pin into the flan. If it comes out clean, the flan is done, but if the egg mixture sticks to it, further cooking is necessary.

Allow to cool, place in the refrigerator and turn out onto a serving dish before bringing to the table.


## Flan de Naranja

Baked Orange Custard

This is a variant of Baked Caramel Custard (see page 106). It is made in small flan moulds – or failing these, in individual cups.

| | |
|---|---|
| 1 egg per person | Caramel (see Baked Caramel |
| 1 orange per person | Custard, page 106) |

Break the egg into a bowl. Wash the orange, grate a little of the peel into a bowl, then squeeze and add all the juice. Beat thoroughly together with the egg and pour into the mould or kitchen cup, previously coated with caramel. Stand the moulds in water and cook and serve as for Baked Caramel Custard (see page 106).


## Huesillos

There is no translation. Flavoured with orange and lemon, they resemble cheese fingers in appearance.

| | |
|---|---|
| 7 oz (200 gm) flour | Grated lemon peel |
| 3½ fl oz (1 dl) olive oil | Grated orange peel |
| 3½ fl oz (1 dl) milk | Olive oil for frying |
| 3½ oz (100 gm) caster sugar | |

Make a dough with all the ingredients, work it until smooth, then shape it, first into small balls and then into fingers with a slit along the top. Fry in hot olive oil, 3 or 4 at a time, until golden.

### *Huevos Flotantes*

Floating Islands

*Serves 4*

| | |
|---|---|
| 4 large eggs | 4 tablespoons caster sugar |
| Salt | Powdered cinnamon |
| 2 pints (1 litre) milk | |

Separate yolks and whites of the eggs and whisk the whites with a pinch of salt until really stiff. Add 3 tablespoons of vanilla-flavoured sugar (see page 106) and beat a little more.

Heat ½ pint (¼ litre) milk in a frying-pan until just simmering – but be careful to regulate the heat to avoid the milk boiling over.

Using two large spoons, take a little of the beaten egg white, shape it like an egg and put it to cook in the milk for a minute or two. As the dollop of egg white cooks and swells, turn it once with a draining spoon, then transfer it to a serving dish. Repeat until all the egg mixture is used up, adding additional milk as required, but without filling the pan too full.

Use the milk and sugar that remain, together with the yolks and a little salt, to make a thin custard. Pour this carefully over the cooked whites, which will rise to the surface. Sprinkle with cinnamon and serve cold.

### *Melocotones al Ron*

Peach Soufflés with Rum

| | |
|---|---|
| 1 egg white per person | Rum |
| Salt | 2 canned peach halves per |
| Caster sugar | person |

Like many Spanish desserts, this is made in individual
dishes. Small *cazuelas* are both practical and decorative;
but the smallest size of ovenproof dish will serve very well.

Beat the egg whites with a little salt until really stiff, then
add a little caster sugar and rum.

Put 2 peach halves on each small dish and divide the
soufflé mixture between them, piling it high with a fork.
Place the dishes in a hot oven (450°F, Mark 8) and cook for
2 to 3 minutes until the mixture turns brown on the top.

Before serving, pour a little warmed rum around each
dish, set alight and bring to the table while still flaming.

### *Melón con Frutas*

Melon Surprise

*Serves 4*

| | |
|---|---|
| 1 melon | 1 small glass maraschino or |
| Fresh grapes, peaches and | other liqueur |
| pears | 2 teaspoons caster sugar |

Cut out and reserve a large wedge from the melon. Remove
and discard the pips, then scoop out the flesh with a large
spoon. Skin and pip the grapes, peel and cut up the other
fruit and mix with the melon flesh. Return this to the
hollowed melon, together with the sugar and maraschino
or other liqueur, replace the cut-out segment and serve ice-
cold from the refrigerator.

### *Pastel de Nueces*

Walnut Flan

*Serves 4*

Caramel (see page 106)
8 oz (200 gm) walnuts
5 eggs, separated
4 oz (100 gm) vanilla-
    flavoured caster sugar
    (see page 106)

4 oz (100 gm) fresh
    breadcrumbs

First make some caramel and coat a flan dish with it exactly
as described for Baked Caramel Custard (see page 106).

Pound the nuts in a mortar. Beat the yolks in a large bowl
and slowly stir in first the sugar and then the nuts. Beat the
egg whites until stiff, fold into the yolks and then fold in the
breadcrumbs.

Pour the mixture into the caramel-coated flan dish, stand
in hot water and cook for an hour in a moderate oven (350°F,
Mark 4) until set – as for Baked Caramel Custard.

### *Tarta de Manzanas*

Open Apple Tart

*Serves 6*

*Pastry*

4 oz (100 gm) unsalted butter
8 oz (200 gm) plain flour
3 teaspoons caster sugar

2–3 tablespoons chilled
    sherry
Milk

Knead the dry ingredients in a bowl with the sherry and a
little water if necessary until they form a ball. Without losing

110

time, line a round 8-inch tart tin with the dough and brush the edge with a little milk.

*Filling*

2 lb (1 kilo) firm eating
  apples, thinly sliced
2 oz (50 gm) unsalted butter
3 tablespoons vanilla-
  flavoured caster sugar
  (see page 106)

1 tablespoon orange juice
Pinch of powdered cinnamon

Melt the butter in a frying-pan, add the apple slices, sprinkle the sugar on top and cook gently until transparent and pale golden, taking care not to break the slices when turning them.

Arrange the apples decoratively in the lined tart tin, and bake in a moderately hot oven (375°F, Mark 5) for 35 minutes.

Reheat the butter left in the pan, add the orange juice and cinnamon, stir and reduce briefly then pour over the tart. Sprinkle over a little more powdered cinnamon and return to the oven for 5 minutes.

Serve with cream.

### Torrijas al Jerez

A traditional Spanish sweet popular with children.

Bread
Egg yolks
Sweet sherry

Olive oil
Icing sugar
Powdered cinnamon

Cut slices of bread (stale bread is perfectly suitable) ½-inch thick and soak for 10 minutes in a mixture of beaten egg yolk and a little sweet sherry, in the proportion of one egg yolk to a slice of bread. Dip into beaten egg and fry crisp in hot olive oil. Sprinkle with icing sugar and cinnamon just before serving.

## Another recipe for Torrijas

Bread                   Olive oil
Eggs                    Icing sugar
Milk                    Powdered cinnamon

Soak slices of bread in a mixture of beaten egg and milk,
leave for 15 minutes. Fry in hot olive oil and sprinkle with
icing sugar and cinnamon as in the previous recipe.


## Tortilla al Ron

Rum Omelette

*Serves 2*

4 eggs                      Knob of butter
1 teaspoon caster sugar     Pinch of salt
1 tablespoon rum

Prepare the eggs and cook as for *Tortilla Azucarada* (see
next recipe), but instead of the lemon peel add a tablespoon
of rum. When the omelet is cooked pour a little more rum
over it and set it alight.
    This can also be made with Kirsch.


## Tortilla Azucarada

Sweet Tortilla

*Serves 2*

4 eggs                  Pinch of salt
Grated lemon peel       Knob of butter
Caster sugar

Separate the yolks of the eggs and stiffly beat the whites.

Add the grated lemon peel, 1 teaspoon sugar and a pinch of salt. Beat a little more, then mix with the yolks.

Melt the butter in an omelet pan and when it is smoking hot pour in the egg mixture and proceed as for a French omelet, folding it when cooked. Sprinkle with more sugar and serve immediately.


## Turrón

Spanish Nougat

*Turrón* is a Spanish sweetmeat typical of a particular time and place. The little wooden boxes, resembling those used for liqueur chocolates, formerly appeared in the shops only at Christmas time. *Turrón* has now been discovered by the tourists and is generally available throughout the year; but it is still made in one place, and one place only – Jijona, in the hills above Alicante.

There are several varieties of *Turrón*, of which the best are *Turrón de Jijona*, a stiff paste made by grinding almonds with egg yolks; and *Turrón de Alicante*. This is a brittle nougat prepared from whole almonds and the whites of eggs. Neither can be made at home with any success; the recipes given in most cook books simply do not work.

There is, however, one type of *Turrón* which can be made without difficulty:


## Turrón de Castañas

Chestnut Nougat

*Serves 4 to 6*

1 lb (½ kilo) chestnuts
3 oz (75 gm) unsalted butter
3 oz (75 gm) cooking
  chocolate, grated

3 oz (75 gm) vanilla flavoured
  caster sugar (see page 106)

113

Use a cake tin with a detachable bottom, so that the finished slab of *Turrón* can be pushed out without using a knife. A suitable size is about 6 inches long, 4 inches wide and 2 inches deep (15 cm × 10½ cm × 5 cm).

Boil the chestnuts. Peel them, pass through a sieve and, while still warm, mix with the butter, grated chocolate and sugar; beat together thoroughly. Smooth the mixture into the cake tin and place in the refrigerator overnight.

The *turrón* will be ready the next day and should be cut into wedges for eating.

# PART TWO
# Marketing and Cooking in Spain

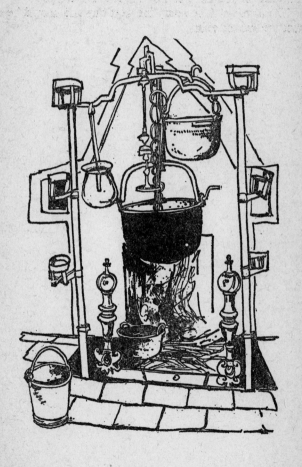

# 11

# Cooking in an Apartment or Villa

Naturally you want to get as much fresh air, sunshine and swimming as possible. Spanish meals being as ample as they are, lunch at a restaurant inevitably results in an overpowering drowsiness – to which the only answer is a siesta and so much less time for acquiring a mahogany tan on the beach. The alternative is a light meal on the terrace; but people who rent villas miss some of the best local food because they do not know what it is, where to look for it, or how to prepare it when they get it.

First a word as to cooking arrangements. Most villas are equipped either with an electric stove or a cooker using butane gas (*gas butano*) in cylinders. Of these, the gas cookers are the more practical, both because the heat is quickly available and because electricity is one of the few things that is expensive in Spain. The gas cylinders normally last for several weeks and are perfectly safe as long as the supply to the cooker is turned off when it is not actually in use.

The days when the taps delivered salt water and the careful visitor brushed his teeth with Vichy water are fortunately past. In the modern apartments the tap water is perfectly safe for drinking and for cooking. This is not always so in the older villas; in which case large earthenware jars (*cántaros*) are provided for storing drinking water from a separate supply. In any case, it is still a wise precaution to have a typhoid injection before going anywhere abroad.

Without the need for cooking at all, Spanish salami (see page 130) and fresh bread make a pleasant lunchtime snack. This can be varied with the highly cured Spanish ham (*Jamón Serrano*) or ordinary ham (*Jamón de York*) available generally at grocers and supermarkets. When working in the fields the Spanish peasants usually take with them a cold Spanish omelet (see page 27), and very good it is for a picnic.

The usual arrangement with rented villas and apartments is for a woman to come in to help with the housework. She may well cope with some simple cooking – a phrase book and sign language can work miracles – but if she proves to be heavy-handed with the olive oil and the garlic, she can still cut out a lot of the drudgery by peeling potatoes, shelling prawns, or cleaning fish.

A fresh salad will go with almost anything and a light meal can be rounded off with fresh fruit and *Manchego* cheese, firm like Cheddar but milder.

Here are some suggestions for quickly prepared lunches. The hot dishes require no more than a frying-pan.

Aranjuez Asparagus (*Espárragos de Aranjuez* see page 89)

Cold Meats Assorted (*Bandeja de Fiambres* page 60)

Fried Fresh Sardines (*Sardinas Fritas* page 56)

Fried Prawns in Shell (*Gambas a la Plancha* page 50)

Fried Spring Chicken (*Pollitos Pequeños Fritos* page 80)

Mixed Fried Fish (*Fritura Mixta de Pescados Pequeños* page 50)

Mussels for an Aperitif (*Mejillones de Aperitivo* page 51)

Russian Salad (*Ensaladilla Rusa* page 89)

Red Pepper Salad (*Ensalada de Pimientos* page 88)

Spanish Omelet (*Tortilla Española* page 27)

Spanish 'Scrambled' Eggs (*Huevos Revueltos con Tomate* page 23)

Toasted Sandwich (*Sandwich Caliente* page 102)

# 12

# Holiday Shopping

When the Spanish woman does her shopping, her first call is at the local market. Every town and village in Spain and Majorca possesses a market in some form. In large places it will be a lofty glass-roofed building divided into sections, each with dozens of small stalls, devoted to fruit and vegetables, meat, poultry, eggs, *embutidos* and so on. The fish market is often housed separately. These large urban markets are normally open every day until 2 PM – except for Sundays and the numerous public holidays.

The villages are more informal. The market proper is held once a week when the stall-holders roll up in antiquated vans and spread their wares, such as clothing, fabrics and earthenware, on trestles in the open air or on the ground. However, on the other days of the week it is usually possible to buy fish and vegetables in the market place, which is often near the church.

When staying within easy driving distance of a town, a periodic visit to the market is well worthwhile because food there is more varied, fresher and cheaper than elsewhere. In any case, the Spanish markets are so colourful that visiting them is as good as going to the cinema.

Fresh fruit, fish, and meat are also available from ordinary shops. The butcher's shop (*carnicería*) presents a barren and denuded appearance, but this is because the supplies are kept in the refrigerator. A price list is usually displayed on the wall – and prices can be high for items in short supply, like steak. Veal, lamb and chicken are the best buys.

Fish can be had in such magnificent variety and abundance all along the Mediterranean coast and in Spain generally, that money is better spent at the fishmonger (*pescadería*). Particularly attractive are the mounded red piles of shellfish (*mariscos*), including prawns (*gambas*) in all shapes and sizes, sea crayfish (*cigalas*), spider crabs (*centollos*), and lobsters (*bogavantes*). Incidentally, no self-respecting Spaniard considers fish to be fresh unless it is sold on the day that it is caught.

Frozen food is not a good buy in Spain and is sold only in the more expensive grocers and supermarkets. Frozen vegetables in particular are virtually unknown, for the very good reason that the Spanish housewife buys fresh vegetables in season at the market, where they are abundant and inexpensive.

Bread is bought at the *panadería*. It is always baked on the premises, and comes crusty, fragrant, and still warm from the oven. The Spaniards do not like eating stale bread and often buy it twice a day.

Spain is famous for its cakes, pastries and chocolates, made fresh every day. These are usually sold, not at the bakery, but at a pastry shop (*pastelería*).

*Pastelerías* and *Confiterías* are two of the few establishments which are *always* open on Sundays. Here are some of the things they sell:

*Tarta Helada*
An iced cake made with sponge, ice cream and nuts

*Helados*
Ice cream

*Borrachos*
*Emparedados* } Small cakes
*Nuris*
*Rusos*

*Petisús*
Eclairs

*Almendras garapiñadas*
Sugar-coated almonds

*Chocolates*
Fresh and hand-made from bitter chocolate, these are delicious in Spain

*Huesos de Santo*
Little marzipan fingers

*Polvorones*
Dry, powdery sweetmeats made from almonds and wrapped in twists of paper. They are sometimes eaten with a glass of sherry

*Membrillo*
Made from the compacted flesh of the quince sweetened with sugar

*Turrones*
Spanish nougat. (For further details see page 113)

*Yemas de Santa Teresa*
A speciality of Avila, though also sold elsewhere, made from egg yolks, sugar and other ingredients

*Yemas de coco*
Also made from egg yolks and flavoured with coconut

*Coca Valenciana*
Though bought at the *pastelerias* in the Valencia region, this is not a sweetmeat, but a savoury tart containing tomato and tuna fish

The *pastelerías* and *confiterías* also sell *embutidos* (see page 130).

Whether eating at home or in a restaurant, the Spaniards usually finish a meal with fresh fruit or, less commonly, cheese.

The fruit is home-grown and therefore eaten only in season. The oranges and tangerines from Valencia and Castellón de la Plana, available from about the beginning of November until March, are of the best. Melons and water-melons are plentiful and cheap during the summer and autumn. The peaches are also very cheap, but the flesh is considerably firmer than that of an English or Italian peach.

The north of Spain produces apples and pears in plenty – also good cider – but the fruit never has the juice or the flavour of the best varieties grown in other countries. On the other hand, the muscatel grapes from the south and the Canary bananas are delicious. Among the exotics, look out for *nísperos* (medlars), *granadas* (pomegranates), and fresh figs, green or black (so cheap they are fed to the pigs!) and best served ice-cold from the refrigerator.

*Useful tip:* never park a car in the shade of a tree bearing ripe figs – they drop and explode like time-bombs!

Apart from the local *Manchego* cheese (see page 119), the *Quesos de Nata* (cream cheeses) and *Queso de Cabrales* (a cheese from the north, somewhat resembling Roquefort), Gruyère-type and Dutch-type cheeses made in Spain are generally available.

*Churros* and the *churrería*, where they are made and sold – often located just outside the market – are a peculiarly Spanish institution. These long, golden-brown fingers, taken straight from the smoking olive oil, are a little like a doughnut, but much lighter. With a cup of hot chocolate or coffee, they are popular for breakfast or for the afternoon *merienda*.

Grocery shops are thick on the ground and are called *ultramarinos* or *colmados*. Apart from the usual groceries and cleaning materials, they carry a wide range of bottled wines and spirits – but wine for everyday drinking can be obtained more cheaply from the *bodega* (see page 141). It is useful to know that many kinds of food often only obtainable elsewhere in packets are available 'loose' in Spain. They are consequently much cheaper. These include breadcrumbs, biscuits, grated cheese, dried herbs and dried vegetables for soups, pasta, olive oil and vinegar. (It is best to buy olive oil in large 5-litre cans or in big bottles. 'Loose' oil sold by the litre is apt to be rough.)

A mundane but important note. Toilet rolls must be purchased at the *ultramarinos*. All other toilet requisites, such as soap, shampoos, toothpaste, suntan oils and beauty preparations are sold in the *perfumería* and not at a chemist proper, the *farmacia*, which deals only in medicines and prescriptions. Most medicines, like sulfaguanidine, so useful for 'Mediterranean tummy', and antibiotics, may be obtained without a prescription.

The new apartment blocks springing up all along the coasts of Spain and Majorca often incorporate a supermarket (*supermercado*). These establishments stock every sort of fresh food (except fish), groceries, wine and spirits, and toiletries. If shopping is not so colourful at a supermarket, it nevertheless saves a great deal of time.

A major preoccupation of every holiday is the dispatch of

picture postcards. Even the large cities boast only a single central post office (*correos*), but stamps can be bought in any tobacco shop (*estanco*). English cigarettes are not easily come by; but the American brands are cheap and plentiful. A good buy at the *estancos* are the domestic Canary cigars, milder than those from Cuba – and much cheaper.

Finally, an establishment which has no place outside Spain is the *horchatería*, most commonly found in the Valencia region. Here they sell a refreshing, milky-looking cold drink, *horchata*. Made from *chufas*, or 'earth almonds', it is a pleasant change from the more usual wine or lager.

# 13

# Cooking Vessels

*Cooking Vessels: Note the* paellera *in centre foreground. To the left is a small* cazuela, *with a larger version behind it*

The *cazuelas* frequently mentioned in the recipe section are made of brown earthenware – a deep red brown like the earth of Spain. They can be bought all over Spain in shops, village stores, and street markets and come in sizes ranging from the small individual *cazuela* suitable for making *huevos a la flamenca* (see page 22) to a huge oval dish large enough for roasting a shoulder of lamb, and in all depths from the shallow dishes used for *canalones* (see page 96) and fish in sauce, to pots capacious enough to make a stew for a family of twelve.

Originally made from the only available material, *cazuelas* have been used since the time of the Moors – and probably before. Their use has persisted because they are designed for simmering food on a low wood or charcoal fire and also for serving the meal. Apart from their decorative appearance and heat-retaining qualities, they are still the best cooking vessels because they preserve the flavour of the ingredients better than pots and pans made of metal.

In addition to this, they are the cheapest casseroles or pots on the market in Spain, costing from about 5 pesetas for a small *cazuelita* to a maximum of 35 pesetas for the giant sizes. Most rented villas and apartments are equipped with earthenware cooking pots; if not, it is worth buying them for the small amount that they cost, for use during the stay.

Here is a tip for fireproofing a new *cazuela*. Take two or three cloves of garlic and rub them thoroughly over the unglazed base of the vessel. Once the juice has been absorbed, fill the *cazuela* with water and bring it slowly to the boil. Throw the water away and the *cazuela* is ready for use.

The very large flat *cazuelas* are sometimes used for making *paella*, but the round metal *paelleras*, now available in specialized kitchen shops and ironmongers abroad, are really more practical for this purpose. The heat is more evenly distributed and the handles make it easier to shake the ingredients during cooking.

# 14
# Spanish Ham and Salami

The name given to ham and the many varieties of cured pork and sausage is *embutidos*. These hams and the dark red, dried-up-looking sausages can be seen hanging from the ceiling in any Spanish grocer's or pork meat shop (*charcutería*).

The sausages, mostly smoked and spiked with herbs and sweet paprika, can either be eaten cold or put to various culinary uses.

All these products originate from *La Matanza*, an annual rite established centuries ago. In all the villages of Spain and the Balearic Islands, the family, however poor, keeps a pig which is fed from scraps or left to forage. The best *embutidos* traditionally come from the Portuguese border, where the animals feed on acorns from the oak forests.

Once a year, just before Christmas, the owners invite their friends and relatives to *La Matanza* (The Killing of the Pig). After the man of the house has felled the pig, by this time enormous, the womenfolk immediately set to, making use of every part of it as rations for the hard winter months ahead. The legs are cut off for curing; and everything else is made into sausage in some shape or form. Together with cold *tortilla, chorizo, jamón* and *tocino* are what the shepherds and labourers take with them when they leave for the day's work in the fields and mountains.

The varieties of *embutidos* are endless; here are some of the more familiar:

### Jamón Serrano
A dark, highly-cured ham reminiscent of *Jambon de Bayonne*. With or without fresh melon it is excellent as a starter.

### Jamón de York
This is simply ham cured in the usual British way.

### Tocino
Nothing similar to British or Danish bacon is obtainable in Spain. This is the nearest approach. It is very fatty – the name derives from the Arabic *tachim*, meaning fat – but goes well with fried eggs for breakfast.

## Chorizo de Pamplona

One of the most attractive Spanish sausages to eat on its own or with bread, which is the usual custom. It consists of finely chopped pork mixed with paprika, spices, herbs and garlic. This mixture is put into the intestinal skins of the animal and hung up to dry for a very long time. Cut into thin slices, it goes well with a glass of sherry; it can also be used as a piquant ingredient for dishes such as *Huevos a la Flamenca* (see page 22), stews and so on.

## Chorizo de Salamanca

This is made from bigger chunks of ham, again mixed with paprika, garlic, herbs, and spices. It is coarser in texture and has a completely different flavour.

## Chorizo de Catimpalos

Rather similar to *Chorizo de Salamanca*, but prepared in strings of smaller sausages.

## Lomo

This is lean loin of pork compressed into a skin, like ham sausage. It fries well with eggs when cut into thin slices, but is even better uncooked as an aperitif or picnic snack.

## Longanizas

The nearest Spanish equivalent of English pork sausages, these are always fried.

## Salchichas

These look like chipolatas, but the filling is darker and coarser in texture. They must be cooked and are often used for garnishing *paellas* or in stews.

## Morcilla

This is a close equivalent of our black pudding, the German *blutwurst* and the French *boudin*. It may be fried in slices or added to stews and other dishes.

### Sobreasada Mallorquina

Entirely Majorcan in origin, this is a much milder form of pink sausage, flavoured mainly with sweet paprika powder. It spreads like paste and goes excellently with that other Majorcan speciality, the small, tubby, oval Inca biscuit, made to be halved without crumbling. *Sobreasada* also makes very tasty sauces when added to the traditional *sofrito* (see page 6).

# 15
# Useful Words

Spanish names for the cuts of meat most commonly sold are often not listed in the dictionary; and fish often goes by nicknames – for example, near Malaga, there are coarse fish affectionately known as 'cats' and 'dogs', and around Valencia *sopa de dátiles* does not mean 'date soup', but a rich fish stew made from a rare variety of mussel.

The accompanying list may therefore prove useful when shopping in Spain. Any pocket dictionary or phrase book will give you the Spanish words for varieties of fruit and vegetables and things like rice and sugar.

## SHELLFISH (*Mariscos*)

| | |
|---|---|
| *Almejas* | Clams |
| *Bogavante* | Lobster |
| *Camarones* | Shrimps |
| *Cambaro, Cangrejo* | Crab |
| *Centollo* | Spider Crab |
| *Chirlas* | Cockles |
| *Cigalas* | Sea Crayfish (*Arctus ursus*) |
| *Gambas* | Prawns, Scampi |
| *Langosta* | Spring Lobster |
| *Langostinos* | 'Norway Lobster' (*Nephrops norvegicus*) |
| *Mejillones* | Mussels |
| *Ostras* | Oysters |
| *Percebes* | 'Barnacles' (*Pollicipes cornucopia*) |

*Percebes* somewhat resemble detached clusters of lobster's claws; and when the covering is stripped away, the meat also bears some resemblance to lobster. Delicious as an aperitif.

## FISH (*Pescado*)

| | |
|---|---|
| *Anchoas* | Tinned Anchovies |
| *Angulas* | Tiny Eels |
| *Atún* | Tinned Tuna |
| *Bacalao* | Dried Salted Cod |
| *Besugo* | Bream |
| *Bonito* | Fresh Tuna |
| *Boquerones* | Fresh Anchovies |
| *Calamares* | Inkfish, Squid |

134

| | |
|---|---|
| *Chanquetes* | Whitebait |
| *Lenguado* | Sole |
| *Lubina* | Bass |
| *Merluza* | Hake |
| *Mero* | Rock Bass |
| *Pescadilla* | Whiting |
| *Pulpo* | Octopus |
| *Rape* | Angler Fish |
| *Raya* | Skate |
| *Rodaballo* | Turbot |
| *Salmón* | Salmon |
| *Salmonete* | Red Mullet |
| *Sardinas* | Fresh Sardines |
| *Sardinas en Lata* | Tinned Sardines |
| *Trucha* | Trout |

## MEAT (*Carne*)

| | |
|---|---|
| *Carne de Aves* | Poultry |
| ,, ,, *Buey* | Beef |
| ,, ,, *Carnero* | Mutton |
| ,, ,, *Cerdo* | Pork |
| ,, ,, *Cordero* | Lamb |
| ,, ,, *Ternera* | Veal |
| ,, ,, *Vaca* | Cow |
| *Cochinillo Lechal* | |
| *o Tostón Asado* | Sucking Pig |
| *Conejo* | Rabbit |
| *Cordero Lechal* | Baby Lamb |
| *Liebre* | Hare |

Beef is not eaten on anything like the scale in England. Its place is taken by corresponding cuts from the cow.

## CUTS OF MEAT (*Cortes de Carne*)

| | |
|---|---|
| *Bistec* | Beefsteak |
| *Cabeza de Ternera* | Calf's Head |
| *Chuletas de Ternera* | Veal Chops |
| *Entrecote* | Entrecote Steak |
| *Entrecote de Vaca* | Entrecote Steak from the Cow |
| *Escalopas de Ternera* | Veal Escalope |

| | |
|---|---|
| *Espaldilla* | Shoulder |
| *Filetes de Ternera* | Fillets of Veal |
| *Filetes de Cerdo* | ,, ,, Pork |
| *Filetes de Vaca* | ,, ,, Cow |
| *Jamón* | Ham |
| *Lomo de Cerdo* | Loin of Pork |
| *Manos de Cerdo* | Pigs' Trotters |
| ,, ,, *Ternera* | Calves' Feet |
| *Solomillo* | Fillet Steak |
| *Tourneðos* | Tournedos, Tenderloin Steak |

## EDIBLE OFFAL (*Menudillos*)

| | |
|---|---|
| *Callos* | Tripe |
| *Hígado* | Liver |
| *Higadillos de Pollo* | Chicken Livers |
| *Lengua* | Tongue |
| *Riñones* | Kidneys |
| *Sesos* | Brains |

Edible offal may be bought at the village butcher, but in the large markets it is sold only at special stalls.

## POULTRY AND GAME (*Aves y Caza*)

| | |
|---|---|
| *Alondras* | Larks |
| *Capón* | Capon |
| *Cordonices* | Quails |
| *Gallina* | Boiling Fowl |
| *Pato* | Duck |
| *Pavo* | Turkey |
| *Perdices* | Partridges |
| *Pichones* | Pigeons |
| *Pollo* | Chicken |

*A note in time*. If you find yourself in a Spanish restaurant and want to ensure that no garlic comes your way, issue firm instructions to the waiter that you want your food to be cooked *sin ajo* – 'without garlic'. And should you object to olive oil, ask for your food to be cooked with butter – (*mantequilla*) – and not oil (*aceite*). (We cannot answer for the outburst that this will provoke – or the outcome. At least you have tried!)

# PART THREE
# Spanish Wines

*Sherry*

The shipping of white wines to England from the area of Jerez de la Frontera in the extreme south of Spain – from which sherry takes its name – was well established in the sixteenth century and has continued, with temporary interruptions, ever since.

British interest in the drinking, shipping and making of sherry is reflected in the names of the great sherry concerns: Williams & Humbert, Duff Gordon, Osborne, Sandeman, and Gonzales Byass – to mention but a few. The sons of the sherry dynasties still go to Eton; and the wives and daughters still congregate for 'afternoon tea' at the *Los Cisnes* Hotel in Jerez de la Frontera – but at 8 PM.

A great deal has been written about the complex business of making sherry; and those interested will find excellent accounts in H. Warner Allen's *Sherry and Port*, London, 1952, or in the more recent *Sherry*, by Julian Jeffs, London, 1970.

Sherry is not, of course, a 'natural' wine but is made by a process of blending and fortification with grape spirit. In the first place the wine owes its character to the *palomino* and *Pedro Ximénez* grapes, from which it is principally made, and to the chalky white soil on which they are grown. After picking, the grapes are laid out on esparto grass mats to lose some of their moisture, treated sparingly with gypsum and crushed. The liquid is then poured into oaken casks to ferment.

This stage is the beginning of the years-long process of sampling and blending the fermenting musts. The process is entirely dependent on the skill of the *capataz*, or head cellarman. His task requires great expertise, since butts of apparently similar young wine mature very differently and lend themselves to the making of sherries of quite distinct type.

Whatever the final style of the sherry, it is produced in a *solera*. This is a tiered arrangement of hundreds upon hundreds of oak butts, housed in cool, airy, cathedral-like *bodegas*. A limited amount of wine from the oldest row of butts is from time to time drawn off for blending and bottling, these butts then being replenished or 'refreshed' with rather younger wine, which is progressively made good from a series of still younger butts forming the 'scales' of the complete *solera*. The great advantage of this involved system, described here only in principle, is that it makes possible the production of sherries that are completely dependable and true to type, so that one bottle of 'La Ina' or 'Tio Pepe' is exactly like another.

The end products of the process can be divided into three basic classes of sherry: *fino*, *palo cortado* and *oloroso*. These are progressively darker and fuller-bodied.

*Fino* is the palest, lightest and most delicate of sherries. When aged in casks, it gains in colour and body, developing into *amontillado*, with its characteristic 'nutty' flavour and depth of bouquet.

*Palo cortado* is a rare wine, most difficult to make and correspondingly expensive, if genuine. Its deep bouquet and clean, fresh flavour make it the delight of the connoisseur.

*Olorosos*, though dry in the natural state, are often blended and sweetened to produce the 'cream' sherries so popular as dessert wines.

*Manzanilla*, made not in Jerez de la Frontera, but in Sanlucar de Barrameda a few miles to the north-west, where the Guadalquivir estuary opens into the Atlantic, is often described by enthusiasts as having the fresh tang of its native sea breezes. This is perhaps poetic licence, but *manzanilla* is nevertheless the driest and one of the most aromatic of sherries.

A number of the sauces and other recipes given in this book call for a small amount of sherry. By this is meant sherry and not sherry-type wine from South Africa or Cyprus. It is as much a false economy to prepare *riñones al Jerez* with cooking sherry as to attempt *boeuf à la bourguignonne* with a rough red wine.

### Spanish Brandy

This is another product of Jerez de la Frontera and Sta Maria del Puerto nearby. In Spain it is surprisingly both less expensive and more widely drunk than sherry and when mixed with soda makes a pleasant aperitif.

It is usually made from grape spirit supplied from the distilleries of the La Mancha region to the north. This is further distilled and diluted with water; flavouring essences are added, and it is then aged in old sherry butts of American oak. The *solera* used for a good Spanish brandy may employ as many as 16 'scales'.

It is perhaps a pity that it should generally be labelled *coñac*, because it possesses an individuality of its own and is by no means an imitation of the French *cognac*. Spanish brandy is a lively, full-flavoured liquor, and it is easy to acquire a taste for it. Apart from a number of somewhat caramalized brandies popular in Spain, there are drier varieties like 'Fundador' and 'Soberano'. Of the more expensive *coñacs*, 'Magno' is darker, more full-bodied, smoother, and a little sweeter. More expensive still, 'Carlos Primero' is paler, lighter, more fragrant, a bit sugary, but more after the style of a French *cognac*.

By distilling the *orujo*, or residue of pips and skins from wine-making, the Spanish also produce *aguardiente*. This is a colourless, highly alcoholic spirit analogous to the French *marc de Bourgogne*.

### Table Wines

Thanks to the sunny and reliable summers, vineyards flourish the length and breadth of the country and Spaniards drink *vino corriente* (ie *vin ordinaire*) with every meal. Even small children will take a glass of red wine, often mixed with a little water.

Because the drinking of wine with meals is universal and because the wine they drink is so cheap, Spaniards generally are much less fussy about names and vintages than the English. The traditional source of supply is the local *bodega*, stone-flagged and redolent of heady, vinous vapours. The casks are lined against the wall, and their contents, mostly of local origin, are tersely described in such terms as *clarete* (red), *tinto* (a heavier red wine), *blanco* (white), or *vino rancio* ('old wine' – often a white wine half way in strength to sherry). Chalked on the casks is the alcoholic strength in degrees and the price in pesetas per litre. Empty bottles or wicker-covered jars must be provided for replenishment; corks are free.

With the march of tourism, the Spaniards are taking enthusiastically to supermarkets. The wine most widely sold in them is produced at large local agricultural cooperatives and sold in litre bottles. Such, for example, is Cariñena, grown near Zaragoza and available as *tinto*, *clarete* and *blanco*.

Apart from the hundreds of different brands of sherry, Spanish brandy and liqueurs, the supermarkets, and particularly the high-class grocers, sell a wide range of *vinos de marca* or *vinos embotellados* (bottled wine). It would be wrong to describe these as vintage wines in the sense of a French claret or Burgundy grown on a vineyard running to a maximum of a few hundred acres. Nevertheless, they are the cream of the Spanish table wines, mostly from the upland valleys of the Rioja district around Logroño in the north of Spain, where the soil and the climate are specially favourable.

In contrast to the hundreds of *châteaux* and *domaines* in the Bordeaux and Burgundy districts, there are only thirty-eight Bodegas entitled to *export* wines with the *denominacion de origen Rioja* (a guarantee corresponding to the French *appellation d'origine*). To supplement the fruit from their own vineyards, they buy grapes from independent farmers and also cooperative-made wine for blending. By no means all of the 100,000 acres of vineyards in the Rioja produce fine wines, but typical concerns like Federico Paternina or the Bodegas Bilbainas operate on the largest scale.

Whatever their historical origin, the grapes used in making fine Riojas – and they have been making wine in Rioja since Roman times – long ago became indigenous to the region. Those regularly employed are, for red wines, *Tempranillo*, *Graciano*, *Mazuelo* and *Garnacho;* and for white, *Malvasia* and *Viura*. Perhaps the best of the Riojas are the lighter red wines, made by allowing only limited contact with the skins during fermentation and often described as Rioja-clarete – though to compare Riojas either with claret or Burgundy seems a mistake, since they are wines with a distinct style and character of their own.

As a class, and irrespective of the year of vintage, Riojas are remarkably consistent in quality, both because of the usual predictability of the weather and the large scale of the wine-making operation, and because Government regulations require that they be matured in oak casks for at least two years.

Still, there *are* vintage Riojas, for example, *Cosecha 1955* means Vintage 1955. It is the practice to mature the wine much longer in cask than is the case in France – arguably, modern French wines spend too little time in the wood and too long in the bottle, and vice versa in Spain. Wine in casks is occasionally 'refreshed' by the addition of wine from later vintages to make good any loss of volume from evaporation. Beyond this, wine that has been set aside to mature in the oak *barríca* is not blended.

The Marqués de Riscal, the Marqués de Murrieta, and certain other Bodegas in the case of their best wines regularly identify the vintage; but a much commoner method of labelling Rioja is with some such description as *Embotellado en su quinto año* – without mention of a year – which means that the wine in question has been bottled in the fifth year after the harvest.

For the connoisseur, there is one rare Spanish wine which is in a class of its own and which most approximates to a French *premier cru*. Vega Sicilia, with its baby brother Valbuena, is grown on a small estate nestling beside the Duero river in Old Castile. It is heady to a degree with a cedar-wood fragrance reminiscent of port; and a sample of Valbuena recently analysed in London was found to contain no less than $16 \cdot 5\%$ of alcohol by volume.

There is a story that Sir Winston Churchill, a great claret fancier, was served a bottle of Vega Sicilia in the course of an elaborate banquet at the Spanish Embassy in London. He singled it out from all the other wines on a choice list, reportedly saying, 'my vote goes to this unknown French wine'.

After the native growths had been destroyed by that insect

143

pest of the vine, phylloxera, towards the end of the nineteenth century, Vega Sicilia was indeed replanted with French vines – grafted, of course, on to resistant stocks. In acclimatizing the plants to the conditions of the Duero valley, Don Eloy Lecanda and his successors have succeeded in producing altogether unique wines. Only in tiny vineyards, such as that belonging to the Marqués de Riscal, producing wine for private consumption, and outside the commercial operation of the Bodega, are French grapes otherwise grown in Spain.

For the great majority of Spaniards, the choice *vinos de marca* remain on the shelves of the grocer or on the wine lists of the restaurants, delights reserved for high days and feasts or for the foreign tourist. They habitually drink a convivial glass of *blanco* in the *taberna* before a meal, and *tinto* with food. Spaniards do not make a great point of drinking red wine with meat and white with fish or fowl. There is good reason for this in that most Spanish or Majorcan dishes are so highly seasoned that the best accompaniment is a strong red wine. To drink white wine with that best known of fish and chicken dishes, *paella*, would merely strike the Spaniard as insipid.

A popular and most refreshing drink in hot weather is *sangría*. This is made by pouring a bottle of ordinary red wine into a large jug and adding a lot of ice cubes, sliced orange and lemon, a sherry glass of Spanish brandy and a sprig of fresh mint.

### A Short Wine List

The following notes have been prepared for visitors who wish to experiment with something more than *vino corriente* and want to find their way about a wine list. But there is only one rule about wine drinking in Spain – to drink what you like with your food and to enjoy it.

### Alella

These soft, fruity, full-flavoured wines, red and white, come from vineyards in the Barcelona region first established by the Romans. It is possible to obtain a dry white Alella, but the well-known Marfil *blanco*, though fresh and luscious, tends to be sweet to the British taste.

## Chacolí
*Vino verde* (a 'green' or young wine) from the Basque provinces of the Atlantic coast. Best drunk on the spot, it is dry and available both as red and white.

## Málaga
A famous sweet dessert wine made from Muscatel and Pedro Ximénez grapes.

## Montilla
This white wine, produced in the Córdoba area of Andalucía, is light, dry and sherry-like. It is not fortified like sherry, but can nevertheless be drunk as an aperitif.

## Sparkling Wines
Though the best of the Spanish sparkling wines or *espumosos*, like Codorniú (from San Sadurní de Noya south-west of Barcelona), Conde de Caralt and Royal Carlton, are made by the original Champagne method, they may not, as the result of a legal action, be described as 'Spanish Champagne'. They are nevertheless good sparkling wines available in various styles, the driest being labelled *bruto* (French *brut*). Another acceptable and less expensive sparkling wine is Perelada from the foothills of the Pyrenees, made in bulk by the *cuvée close* system. It is greatly superior to the *vinos gasificados* (prepared in the manner of 'fizzy' lemonade by pumping carbon dioxide gas into still white wine), which have little to recommend them except their cheapness.

## Tarragona
The wine traditionally known as Tarragona in Britain, and now not as popular as it once was, is a rough red, somewhat sweetened and fortified with grape spirit.

Of rather more interest, the red table wines from Priorato near Tarragona have a following in Spain and resemble a rather heavy Rioja. Much of the wine from the Tarragona area is used for making vermouth and liqueurs under licence from the well-known houses in France and Italy. The Tarragona-made Chartreuses, for example, are made by the same Carthusian Order of monks from the identical recipes used in Grenoble.

## Valdepeñas

A name loosely applied to the strong but refreshingly dry red wines grown in the very extensive vineyards of La Mancha in New Castile to the south of Madrid, of which the town of Valdepeñas is the centre for the wine trade. This vast and arid plateau, with its occasional windmill silhouetted against the skyline, is Don Quixote country. It produces very drinkable wine in enormous bulk, which is sent to all parts of Spain – most of the excellent carafe wine in Madrid is Valdepeñas – and also shipped abroad, generally for blending or for sale under brand labels. So great is the amount made that in centres like Tomelloso, a portion of it is distilled for use in making Spanish brandy, or simply converted into industrial alcohol.

## Wines of the Rioja

### Rioja

As already remarked, these are the aristocrats of Spanish wines. The following list of some of the principal Rioja Bodegas and their currently available wines is representative, but far from exhaustive. If the bracketed comments read after the fashion of a wine merchant's catalogue, this is to give a rough idea of the type and price range of the wines to those unfamiliar with them. Descriptions such as 3° Año denote the period spent in the *crianza* (or nursery, as the Spanish charmingly have it) – meaning in the above instance that the wine was bottled in its third year.

### Bodegas Bilbainas

Red    Ederra clarete (inexpensive, but very drinkable)
        Villa Paceta (distinctive and more mature)
        Villa Zaco (6° *Año*, a superior dry wine with a good bouquet)

Castel Pomal (6° *Año*, more full bodied)
Reserva
Vendimia Especial } (higher-priced vintage Riojas)

White    Ederra blanco
Viña Paceta (dry)
Cepa de Oro (semi-sweet)
Brillante (sweet)
Dry England (the white wine from Villa Zaco)

Imperator (a good rosé)

*Bodegas Franco Españolas*
Red      Clarete (3° *Año*)
Rioja Bordon (8° *Año*, a heavier wine)
Royal (8/9° *Año*, excellent as befits its age)

White    Castil-Corvo (dry)
Viña Sole (dry, fruity)
Diamante (sweet)

Rosado (dry rosé)

*Bodegas Riojanas*
Various wines, red and white.

*Bodegas Rioja Santiago*
Red      Yago (4° *Año* and 8° *Año*)
Yago Condal (older vintage wines)
Enologica (Año 1904 – a rarity)

White    Yago wines ranging from very dry to sweet

Rosado (rosé)

*Compañía Vinícola del Norte de España* (CUNE)
Red      CUNE (3° *Año* and 4° *Año*)
Imperial Reserva (15° *Año*, a fine Rioja)
Viña Real Plata (4° *Año*, full-bodied)

White    Monopole (extra dry)
        CUNE (4° *Año*, dry)
        Corona 'Semi' (sweet)

*Federico Paternina*
Red     Banda Azul (3° *Año*, a favourite inexpensive Rioja
          in Spain)
        Banda Roja 'Viña Vial' (6° *Año*)
        Gran Reserva (an excellent vintage wine)

White    Banda Dorada (dry, rather reminiscent of Meursault)
        Monte Haro (sweet)

        Banda Rosa (dry rosé)

*López de Heredia*
Red     Various wines, all with a characteristic acidity
        Viña Tondonia Grandes Reservas (distinguished
          vintage Riojas)

White    A range of white wines

        Tondonia Rosada (dry rosé)

*Marqués de Murrieta*
Red     Etiqueta Blanca (5° *Año*, mellow and fruity)
        Ygay Reserva (Vintage 1950)
        Reservas, Castillo Ygay (expensive and splendid
          old vintage wines)

White    Murrieta (one of the best of the reasonably-priced
          white Riojas)

        Rosado (a first-rate dry rosé)

*Marqués de Riscal*
Red     Riscal (4° *Año*, dry, light)
        Reservas (choice vintage wines)

Rosé    Vino Rosado (one of the best Spanish rosés)

Any of the wines from the above Bodegas can be bought with confidence, as indeed Riojas generally bearing the stamp of the *Consejo Regulador*. The red Riscal and both the red and white Murrieta, rather more expensive than some of the others, are particularly highly esteemed in Spain – and with justice. But it would be invidious to say that they are superior to various of the wines in the higher-price bracket from the other concerns. For example, the Paternina Gran Reserva and C.V.N.E. Imperial are undoubtedly among the best of the normally available red Riojas and good wines even by the standard of a château-bottled Bordeaux.

### Spanish Wines Abroad

In no country in the world, outside Spain, is a wider range of sherries available than in the United Kingdom. In fact, more sherry is drunk in this country than in Spain itself. This is perhaps because sherry seems to taste better when drunk in a cold climate than in a warm one.

The position as regards Spanish table wines is very different. It is an exceptional wine store or off-licence which offers more than a choice of an ordinary red wine and a sweet white. These are usually sold in bottles decorated with colourful brand labels, but giving no clue as to the origin of the wine or any guarantee as to its consistency. The likelihood is that it has been produced and blended in bulk in the La Mancha, Alicante or Tarragona regions and shipped by tanker. Such wines are perfectly sound, and for someone who asks no more than that they should be drinkable and alcoholic, they provide an inexpensive answer.

The pity is that this large-scale merchandising operation has created the impression that Spain has nothing better to offer in the way of table wines.

It is possible to buy bodega-bottled Riojas outside Spain, and most delicious they are – but more common practice is for the wine to be shipped in cask and then bottled by the shipper. Where the wine is simply labelled Rioja without the name of the grower, it is a matter of relying on the reputation of the shipper – as in the case of a corresponding bottle of Médoc or Beaujolais. The better Riojas are often bottled under the characteristic label of the Spanish grower. To protect the customer, and as with vintage Bordeaux bottled outside France, the custom is to supply only a sufficient number of labels to the shipper to cover the contents of the casks. A small facsimile stamp on the label and sometimes a separately affixed coloured map of the Rioja region will ensure that the wine is genuine.

# *Index*

154

155

# Cookery and Home Management

# Gardening

# *Sports and Pastimes*

These and other PAN Books are obtainable from all booksellers and newsagents. If you have any difficulty please send purchase price plus 7p postage to PO Box 11, Falmouth, Cornwall.

While every effort is made to keep prices low, it is sometimes necessary to increase prices at short notice. PAN Books reserve the right to show new retail prices on covers which may differ from those advertised in the text or elsewhere.